Careers for You Series

McGraw-Hill's

CAREERS FOR

HARD HATS

& Other Construction Types

MARJORIE EBERTS
MARGARET GISLER

SECOND EDITION

New York Chicago San Francisco Lisbon London Madrid Mexico City
Milan New Delhi San Juan Seoul Singapore Sydney Toronto

The **McGraw·Hill** Companies

Library of Congress Cataloging-in-Publication Data

Eberts, Marjorie.
    Careers for hard hats & other construction types / by Marjorie Eberts &
Margaret Gisler — 2nd ed.
       p. cm. — (McGraw-Hill careers for you series)
    Rev. ed. of: Careers for hard hats & other construction types / Margaret Gisler,
Marjorie Eberts. ©2001.
    Includes bibliographical references.
    ISBN 0-07-154538-7 (alk. paper)
    1. Vocational guidance—United States. I. Gisler, Margaret. II. Gisler,
Margaret. Careers for hard hats & other construction types. III. Title.

HF5382.U5G53 2008
331.702—dc22   2008022934

1 2 3 4 5 6 7 8 9 10 11 12 13 14 15 16 17 18 19 20 DOC/DOC   0 9 8

ISBN 978-0-07-154538-9
MHID   0-07-154538-7

McGraw-Hill books are available at special quantity discounts to use as premiums
and sales promotions or for use in corporate training programs. To contact a
representative, please visit the Contact Us pages at www.mhprofessional.com.

This book is printed on acid-free paper.

This book is dedicated to Matt,
who wore a hard hat for many years;
to Bill, who is now wearing a hard hat
on the job every day; and to Maria
and Larry, who work for a company
that builds equipment used by
hard-hat wearers.

Contents

Acknowledgments

W e wish to thank Kevin Crider for his substantial help in the writing of this edition of *Careers for Hard Hats & Other Construction Types*. We also wish to thank Mary McGowan and Maria Olson for their help in writing the first edition of this book.

We also deeply appreciate the help of all the people who let us write about their careers as hard-hat wearers.

Acknowledgments

Hard-Hat Careers

M iners, oil drillers, loggers, utility workers, and construction
workers have different job responsibilities. Their skills are
vastly different; their work environments are challenging
and often demanding. But they have one thing in common—hard
hats! Millions of people put on a hard hat every day when they go
to work. Drive by a construction site and you'll immediately
notice that everyone is wearing a hard hat. No miner ever enters a
mine without first putting on a hard hat, and every worker building a road has on a hard hat. Utility workers, whether they are
climbing poles or bringing water into a new home, wear hard hats
on the job. The logger wielding a chain saw in the woods has on a
hard hat, and so does the assembly-line worker putting bumpers
on cars. Oil drillers wear hard hats as they bore deep into the
earth. Whenever there is a job where any possible danger of injury
to the head exists, workers wear hard hats for protection.

In ancient times, job safety was not a matter of public concern.
Accidents were accepted as inevitable. Not until the nineteenth
century did great concern emerge about safety at work. Today,
workers can go about their jobs with greater confidence that they
will not be injured because the workplace has become safer due to
the actions of employers, safety legislation, and the wearing of
protective gear—including hard hats.

Is a Hard-Hat Career Right for You?

If some of these hard-hat jobs sound appealing, you can easily tie
your own personal interests to an exciting career. Nature lovers

can become foresters, while adventurers can enjoy searching throughout the world for oil. Car buffs can build automobiles, while those who are fascinated by planes can actually construct them. Even though hard-hat wearers work in very different jobs, they all have some common characteristics. Answer the following questions to see if you are like most construction types.

1. Are you safety conscious? Many hard-hat jobs present dangers for careless workers.
2. Are you willing to follow safety rules? All hard-hat jobs require strict adherence to safety regulations.
3. Do you have the stamina to do physically demanding work? Many hard-hat jobs require considerable lifting, bending, and stooping.
4. Are you willing to work in such adverse conditions that would require you to be at great heights, in confined spaces, or outdoors in all kinds of weather? Many hard-hat jobs present these challenges.
5. Are you flexible? Many hard-hat jobs require you to handle more than one job.
6. Are you a good team worker? In these jobs, you will often have to work closely with others.
7. Are you willing to get additional training beyond high school? Many hard-hat jobs require special training at technical and community colleges and in industry-sponsored classes.
8. Are you willing to work different shifts? This is often a requirement—you may work from 8 A.M. to 4 P.M., 4 P.M. to midnight, or midnight to 8 A.M.
9. Are you willing to work in remote locations? Some hard-hat jobs are located far from cities.
10. Are you comfortable with utilizing technology? Many jobs involve the use of computers and other high-tech equipment.

A Quick Look at Hard-Hat Jobs

When you begin your search for a job, the task may seem daunting as there are so many possibilities. You could drive a bulldozer, work in a steel mill, install elevators, build brick walls, mine for gold, tear down buildings, turn logs into lumber, drill for oil offshore, or do hundreds of other things. As you read this book, you'll soon discover that wearing a hard hat on the job can often be an opportunity to do very exciting work.

This book is designed to help you build a satisfying career in the world of hard hats. Here is a bird's-eye view of some of the careers detailed in this book.

Building Roads, Freeways, and Streets

Even though the United States has one of the greatest networks of roads in the world, we are still building more interstates, highways, and streets every year to satisfy our demand to travel more easily from place to place. Our need for new and better roads creates jobs for those who build and repair them. And in the future, road builders may be installing all kinds of technological innovations that will let us drive on electronic highways.

Many of today's jobs in road building involve the operation of heavy equipment such as bulldozers, scrapers, paving machines, loaders, shovels, trucks, and excavators. Other road-related jobs require general laborers, flaggers, and mechanics. In addition, each job has construction superintendents making sure that all the work is being done correctly and civil engineers who oversee the entire construction project. Road building has jobs for everyone, from those who didn't finish high school to college graduates.

Constructing Houses and Other Buildings

Workers wearing hard hats build the homes where we live, the restaurants where we eat, the factories and offices where we work, and the schools where we learn. New buildings of all kinds are continually being constructed in all parts of the country, and older ones often need remodeling. The construction of buildings is big business—hundreds of billions of dollars are spent on building projects each year.

While some unskilled workers are hired in constructing buildings, most workers are skilled craftspeople. In fact, these hard-hat workers are the largest group of crafts workers in the United States. If you want to construct buildings, you can find a job as a carpenter, bricklayer, stonemason, electrician, plumber, pipe fitter, or structural and reinforcing ironworker. All of these jobs require special training through an apprenticeship or on-the-job training.

Jobs in the Mining Industry

Mining is an important industry that provides us with many of the minerals we use daily: coal for heating, gravel for roads, iron for making cars, copper for wiring, and gold for jewelry. It is also an industry in which working conditions can sometimes be dangerous. Perhaps, as a result, miners are among the highest-paid workers of any industry—and they all wear hard hats.

More than 250,000 workers in the United States are miners, with close to 100,000 of them working in coal mines. If your image of a miner is that of a pick-wielding worker, think again. Miners today operate sophisticated machinery. And while a high school diploma will open the door to the majority of mining jobs, more and more mining jobs require advanced technical training.

Careers in Manufacturing

The word *manufacturing* is related to the Latin words *manus* (hand) and *facere* (to make). Today, however, manufacturing is increasingly accomplished with the help of machinery. And factory workers in the United States make more products of every imaginable type than their counterparts in any other country. Manufacturing is such an important industry in this country that it provides one out of every seven jobs. Manufacturing jobs exist in every area of the country and within small, medium, and large companies.

Not all workers in manufacturing plants need hard hats. Still, they are required equipment for most of the jobs involved in the manufacture of heavy goods such as locomotives, tractors, airplanes, automobiles, and steel products.

Jobs in the Lumber Industry

Logging operations have changed greatly since the days when trees were cut down by loggers swinging axes and crying "Timber!" Most logging is now performed by small crews of three to six workers who use machines to cut trees and haul them from the forest.

Being a logger is not your only option if you want a career working in the forest. Foresters, for example, inventory trees, oversee logging operations, supervise tree planting, and manage public forests and parks. While most loggers can still learn their work through on-the-job training, foresters need to have a bachelor's degree.

While loggers cut down trees, it is the sawmill workers who turn those trees into the lumber used for building and for a variety of wood products. If you have a technological bent, you might want to consider a career in this area, as computers and lasers are commonplace in sawmills, and even more exciting uses of technology are on the horizon.

Jobs in the Petroleum Industry

The petroleum industry has three distinct areas in which you could find a hard-hat job. In exploration jobs, you would be part of a team searching throughout the world for oil and gas. Most exploration jobs require a college, community college, or technical school degree. The majority of hard-hat jobs in the petroleum industry involve the drilling and extracting of oil and gas. Oily tools and the possibility of oil spills and fires make these jobs potentially hazardous, and considerable lifting could be required. As with working in exploration, drilling for oil is a team effort.

The remaining job area in the petroleum industry is in refining oil into gasoline, heating oil, and petrochemical products. Most of the operations jobs in refineries have become mechanized and are overseen in control rooms, but maintenance, repair, inspection, and laborer jobs require hard hats and protective glasses.

Jobs in the Utility Sector

Choose a hard-hat job with a utility company and you will perform an essential service to the public. These services include supplying electricity, natural gas, water, sewage disposal, and telephone services. Utilities owned by private companies tend to be large companies, while those owned by citizens and other citizen-based organizations, such as local municipalities, are usually smaller. The federal government also owns some power plants.

Because each utility offers a different range of jobs, the skills you gain in working for one utility may not transfer to another one. Many of the jobs are outdoors, such as installing and maintaining pipelines and power lines. You can use your high school diploma to find an entry-level job with a utility and then take part in apprenticeship programs to climb a company's career ladder.

More Hard-Hat Careers

In this chapter, we describe even more jobs for hard-hat wearers—some unusual and others quite familiar. We suggest that you add to our list by noting the activities of people you encounter who wear hard hats. You might see an environmental engineer testing a polluted stream, a warehouse worker transporting products on a pallet, or someone high in the air trimming trees.

Education and Training Requirements

Many hard-hat jobs only require graduation from high school for entry-level positions. However, advancing in the company often requires training offered through company and industry classes as well as apprenticeships. Completing job-specific classes at community or technical colleges makes it even easier to win a hard-hat job and to advance once you have started working. Some jobs require a bachelor's degree.

The right educational background is not the only prerequisite for getting a job as a hard hat. For most jobs, you must have the stamina to spend your days doing physical work. And, above all else, you must truly want a job in which you face certain hazards in the workplace that require you to wear a hard hat.

Finding a Job

The traditional ways for finding jobs are especially effective for discovering openings for hard-hat positions. Newspapers routinely advertise vacancies. Many workers also obtain jobs by applying directly to the companies where they wish to work. It is always possible to learn about jobs by talking with workers already employed in an area that appeals to you. Visits to state employment offices can unearth lists of job openings. And, of course, in today's cyber world, you can use the Internet in your job search. Look at company websites, your state's employment website, and any of the employment websites that catalogue all kinds of jobs. Because so many hard-hat jobs exist, you should be able to find one that ties closely to your interests and talents.

CHAPTER TWO

Building Roads, Freeways, and Streets

More than four thousand years ago, Egyptians built the first paved roads. These roads were used to move materials to build the great pyramids. Since then, people have built and paved roads and streets with everything from logs, wood planks, cobblestones, and gravel to the more modern concrete and asphalt.

Today, new technology and materials are used to build longer-lasting and safer roadways. Some roads are being built exclusively for truckers because big trucks ruin roads faster than any other vehicle. The future will bring fascinating roadway innovations, including the electronic highway. This highway will consist of roads programmed to communicate with your car's computer. You will simply tell your car where you want to go, and it will do the navigating and driving for you.

U.S. Roads: An Intricate Network

The United States has the largest network of roads in the world, with more than 4 million of the total 120 million miles of roads and streets around the globe. There are four different kinds of paved roads: interstate highways, arterials, collectors, and local roads and streets. Interstate highways make up about forty-seven thousand miles of roads in this country, and they carry about 25 percent of the traffic. Arterial highways are generally two- and four-lane roads that connect interstate highways with cities. Collector roads connect cities and towns with the arterials, and local roads enable you to get from your home to the grocery store.

Roads in the United States are built and maintained by governments that hire contractors to do the construction. The federal government funds almost 90 percent of the cost for building and maintaining the interstate highway system. State governments are responsible for the arterial and collector roads, while counties, cities, and townships are responsible for their own local roads and streets.

Work Hazards and Conditions

Days are generally long, from eight to ten hours, for everyone involved in building roads, and they can be as long as twelve hours. Most jobs start at 7 A.M. and end about 5 P.M. You may have to work at night or on weekends in order to finish jobs on time and to avoid causing traffic jams.

Weather will affect your workday—rain or snow could shut the job down, and you face working outdoors in the hot summer and the cold winter. In addition, the work environment is frequently noisy, and machines such as jackhammers and concrete saws shake or jolt their operators.

Everyone who works on a road-building site wears a hard hat at all times. Many also wear orange construction vests so they can be seen more easily. That's because building roads is hazardous work if you don't take proper precautions. You are exposed to dangerous situations every day. Heavy equipment operates all around you, and cars and trucks continually pass through the work area. You must watch out for traffic, the rocks and dust that fly up from the heavy equipment, and materials that can fall from trucks and equipment.

The Road Crew

If you are interested in a career building roads, many hard-hat jobs are available. Depending on your skills and level of education, you could find jobs ranging from entry-level traffic flagger with little or no experience to a seasoned area manager. The following chart shows the typical organization of a construction company; the number of people working in each job title depends on the size of the company and the jobs it takes on.

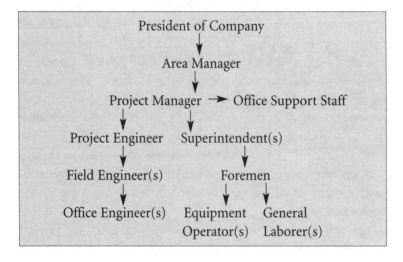

A Foot in the Door: Entry-Level Jobs

You have probably seen flaggers wearing hard hats and bright vests to direct traffic around road construction. This is an entry-level job requiring little to no experience or education. Another entry-level job is the mechanic's helper, who assists mechanics with repairing equipment and by fetching tools, materials, and supplies. Or you could start as a general laborer, who provides much of the physically demanding labor on the construction site. You could excavate tunnels and shafts, dig trenches, mix and place concrete, and set braces to support the excavations. General laborers also may operate a variety of equipment, such as pavement breakers, jackhammers, earth tampers, concrete mixers, guided boring machines, small mechanical hoists, laser beam equipment, and surveying and measuring equipment. General laborers who build bridges are responsible for constructing the bridge deck and for placing supporting beams. They build the forms, place the rebar (reinforcing rods in concrete) and the beams, and pour the concrete.

Job Qualifications and Training

You can get a job as a flagger, a mechanic's helper, or a laborer without work experience or specific training if you are reliable and hardworking. While you will most likely need a high school diploma, not all companies require them. Virtually all employers require that you be at least eighteen years old and physically able to perform the work. You may have to pass a physical examination if your job requires physical exertion. Some employers require drug testing or background checks prior to employment, and periodic random drug testing is becoming more and more common because of the danger involved in handling much of the equipment.

You will learn job skills informally, getting them on the job from more experienced coworkers and your supervisors. As you learn, the opportunity for promotion may present itself. Many construction companies prefer to promote people from within. You could move from general laborer to foreman or even superintendent throughout the course of your career.

Job Outlook and Earnings

In the United States, job growth for entry-level workers in road building is expected to be as steady as the average growth for all occupations. This projected growth is due to the increasing need for new and better roads as well as repairs to prevent deterioration of existing roads. Little threatens the demand for entry-level workers. Technological advances could result in machines replacing certain workers, and job combinations could force more skilled employees to add the duties of general laborers to their own responsibilities. In Canada, job growth is expected to be below average as new technologies improve productivity, which means employers can do more with fewer workers.

In the United States, a general laborer, flagger, or a mechanic's helper earns on average $12.66 per hour. Canadian workers can expect to earn CAN$15.17. What you earn will depend on where you live. Some regions pay far more than others because of a higher cost of living and a tight labor market. Unless you are guaranteed a specific number of paid hours each week, you will be paid only for the hours you work, and, depending on the weather, it may be very many or very few. In some states, unions control the number of hours construction laborers work and help to negotiate salaries with the company. In addition to your hourly wage, some companies offer health care benefits and 401(k) plans, although these benefits are typically reserved for salaried employees.

Equipment Operators

You have probably noted how much machinery is needed to build a road. The terrain has to be raised or lowered to a specific grade, which requires moving large amounts of earth, trees and bushes, rocks, debris, and even garbage. Bridges and overpasses must be built, and new roads must be paved with asphalt or concrete. Behind every piece of road-building equipment is an equipment operator. Most equipment operators work in open cabs, and all of them wear hard hats to protect their heads from flying debris. The operators also wear seat belts, if appropriate. They control their equipment by pushing levers or foot pedals, operating switches, or turning dials, often using complex computers and other technology to help them. Besides running this equipment, the operators often set up and inspect it, make adjustments, and even perform minor repairs when needed. Here is a description of some of the jobs operating road construction equipment:

- **Tractor operator.** Uses a lifting device such as a forklift or a boom.
- **Excavation- and loading-machine operator.** Digs and loads sand, gravel, earth, or similar materials into trucks or onto conveyors.
- **Grader, bulldozer, and scraper operator.** Gouges, distributes, levels, and grades earth with vehicles that have a concave blade across the front; operates trench excavators and other similar equipment.
- **Asphalt-paving-machine operator.** Controls a machine that spreads and levels asphalt for roads; turns valves to regulate the temperature and flow of asphalt onto the roadbed; ensures that the machine distributes the asphalt evenly; ensures a constant flow of asphalt is going into the hopper.
- **Concrete-paving-machine operator.** Moves levers and turns handwheels on the paving machine to lower an attachment that spreads, vibrates, and levels wet concrete within forms; observes the surface of the concrete to point out low spots for workers to add concrete; uses attachments to float the surface of the concrete; sprays on a curing compound; cuts expansion joints.
- **Tamping-machine operator.** Operates a machine that compacts earth and other fill materials for roadbeds; operates a machine with interchangeable hammers to cut or break up old pavement and drive guardrail posts into the earth.
- **Operating engineer.** Operates many kinds of power construction equipment, such as cranes, derricks, shovels, tractors, scrapers, pumps, and hoists. Operating engineers use cranes and derricks to lift materials, machinery, and

other heavy objects from the ground; operate excavation and loading machines equipped with scoops, shovels, or buckets to dig sand, gravel, earth, and similar material and load it into trucks and onto conveyors; drive and control trucks and tractors equipped with a forklift or boom to lift materials; and may also operate and maintain air compressors, pumps, and other power equipment at construction work sites. On bridge jobs, operating engineers may run cranes capable of lifting multiton beams and placing them on supports anywhere from thirty to sixty feet in the air. Most crane operators coordinate their maneuvers in response to hand signals and instructions sent by radio. They often position the loads from onboard consoles or from remote consoles at the site.

Job Qualifications and Training

The equipment used in building roads is expensive. Cranes can cost $1 million, and it is not unusual for bulldozers to cost more than $100,000. It is easy for an inexperienced or unskilled operator to damage this expensive construction equipment. A successful operator needs a good sense of balance, the ability to judge distance, and expert eye-hand-foot coordination. Most construction companies in the United States and Canada require their equipment operators to have a high school diploma. To operate more technologically advanced equipment with computerized controls, you may need more training and some understanding of electronics.

Construction equipment operators usually learn their skills on the job. As a new construction equipment operator, you might be asked to handle light equipment under the guidance of an experienced operator. Some operators train in formal three-year operation-engineer apprenticeship programs administered by unions. These programs consist of at least three years or 6,000 hours of on-the-job training and 144 hours per year of related classroom instruction. Because apprentices learn to operate a wider variety of machines than other entry-level workers, they usually have better job opportunities.

Some private vocational schools offer instruction in the operation of certain kinds of construction equipment. If you complete such a program, it could help you get a job as a trainee or apprentice. However, before you consider such a school, be sure to check its reputation among employers in the area.

Job Outlook and Earnings

In the United States, employment opportunities for construction equipment operators are expected to increase by about 8 percent through 2016. Increased spending on improving the nation's infrastructure of highways, bridges, and dams should result in slightly stronger demand for paving, surfacing, and tamping equipment operators. In addition to general employment growth, many job openings will occur because of the need to replace experienced workers who transfer to other occupations or leave the labor force. In Canada, there is a below average increase in job opportunities for construction equipment operators.

What construction equipment operators earn depends greatly on where they work, what machinery they operate, and the size and nature of the road-building job. Canadian construction equipment operators can expect to earn an average of CAN$22.77 per hour. Pay scales are generally higher in or near big cities and on larger jobs. The annual earnings of equipment operators may be lower than their hourly rates would indicate because the amount of time they work may be limited by bad weather. Table 1 shows recent hourly earnings for the lowest- and highest-paid equipment operators in the United States.

On the Job as a Bulldozer Operator

On a new nine-mile interstate highway under construction in Florida, bulldozer operators arrive on the job ten minutes before their shifts start to check all the oil and fluid levels for their

TABLE 1. Hourly Wages for Equipment Operators

OPERATORS	LOWEST 10%	HIGHEST 10%
Operating engineers	< $11.54	> $30.83
Grading, bulldozer, and scraper operators	< $12.83	> $37.28
Paving, surface, and tamping equipment operators	< $9.97	> $25.30

Source: U.S. Department of Labor, Bureau of Labor Statistics, Occupational Outlook Handbook 2008–2009

machines. Once their dozers are fired up at 7 A.M., the operators begin pushing dirt to build the new highway. Under the direction of a foreman, they push dirt all day long, as fast as possible. In the morning, they work until 11:30 A.M., when they break for lunch. After a half-hour lunch, they work until 4:30 P.M. The only time they stop pushing dirt is during fifteen-minute breaks in the morning and afternoon, but their workdays pass quickly because they are always busy.

During their time on the dozers, operators must always be very alert to what is going on around them to avoid hurting themselves or others. And they wear hard hats at all times to protect themselves from flying debris.

Construction Foremen and Superintendents

The basic difference between a foreman and a superintendent is the level of responsibility. One superintendent may oversee multiple foremen and is ultimately responsible for all of the workers reporting to those foremen. As a foreman or superintendent, you work outdoors in a variety of weather conditions. You need to arrive at the job site before other workers and often stay after others leave. You may work night shifts or even double shifts. Because some companies have reorganized their corporate structures and downsized, many foremen and superintendents today oversee more workers, have more responsibilities, and work longer hours. As a result, they often have more on-the-job stress.

The primary task of a foreman or superintendent is to ensure that workers, equipment, and materials are used in ways that maximize productivity. Part of the job is to make sure that machinery is set up correctly and maintenance work is scheduled. In addition, foremen and superintendents organize workers' activities and make adjustments to ensure that work continues uninterrupted, is performed correctly, and is completed on time. They also must keep production and employee records. Other responsibilities include training new workers and helping create a safe work environment.

Superintendents have more responsibilities than foremen. They serve as the primary pathway for information transferred between management and the general laborers and heavy-equipment operators. They inform workers about company plans and policies; recommend good performers for wage increases, awards, or promotions; and deal with poor performers by outlining expectations, counseling them about proper methods, issuing warnings, or recommending disciplinary action. Superintendents also regularly meet with management to plan construction projects, report any problems, and discuss possible solutions. In companies with labor unions, superintendents must follow all the provisions of labor management contracts.

Computers have dramatically changed the ways foremen and superintendents perform their duties. They now use computers to schedule work flow, monitor the quality of workers' output, keep track of materials, and update the inventory control system.

Job Qualifications and Training

When employers are searching for a new foreman or superintendent, they generally look for experience, job knowledge, organizational skills, and leadership qualities. Other important attributes include the ability to motivate employees, to interact with a diverse workforce, and to maintain a high level of morale. Foremen and superintendents also need solid communication and interpersonal skills.

To become a foreman or a superintendent, you will almost certainly need a high school diploma, and it would be difficult to advance beyond superintendent without one. Many companies provide on-the-job training in human resources, computer software, and management skills.

Job Outlook and Earnings

Employment of foremen and superintendents is sensitive to the short-term nature of many of these jobs. It also depends on the demand for the construction, maintenance, and repair of roads. The median annual earnings for superintendents and some foremen is more than $44,000, with the middle 50 percent earning between $33,800 and $57,300. The lowest 10 percent of foremen and superintendents earns less than $26,000, while the highest 10 percent earns more than $84,000. Most foremen and superintendents earn much more than their workers and are typically salaried employees.

On the Job with a Foreman

Sandy Shaw is a foreman with one of the country's largest heavy-construction companies. His introduction to construction began in a high school vocational education program in masonry. After graduation, Sandy joined the U.S. Navy, where he picked up the ability to manage people—an essential skill for a foreman. At one point in his ten-year navy career, he commanded more than two hundred people. When he left the navy, Sandy performed brickwork for friends, then entered the construction industry to work in a small company with his father-in-law. On his first construction job, Sandy started as foreman of bridge decks, curbs, and gutters. Within a few years, Sandy was promoted to superintendent, then he moved to his present job as a grading foreman with a much larger company.

Sandy has many responsibilities that keep him busy every minute on the job. He meets with the engineers to determine where the utility pipe will go and when it should be placed, and then he directs the crew that lays it. Sandy also builds brick catch basins and builds wood forms so that joints will fit and function properly. Another part of his job is moving equipment into position so that other employees can fuel and service it for the night shift. Sandy also manages paperwork to keep track of the materials used, and he helps with traffic control. On rainy days, he builds forms, works with metal, and helps with anything that needs to be done.

As a salaried employee, Sandy works a guaranteed sixty-hour week. His day typically begins at 6:30 in the morning and ends around 6:30 at night. He works five full days each week and a half day every Saturday, with an occasional Sunday as well. On the job, he keeps an upbeat attitude and, in doing so, has found that others around him are far more cheerful. Sandy would like to become a project manager, and he is ready to return to school to reach this goal.

Career Advice. Sandy says that if you are interested in a career in construction, you need to know how to "work smart, not hard." He advises job seekers to continue with their education and find plenty of hands-on training to make themselves more valuable to future employers.

On the Job with a Superintendent

Constructing bridges is common in roadwork because surface terrains vary so greatly. That means construction sites often need workers who specialize in bridge building, such as Ray Fuentes, a bridge superintendent for a large construction company. Ray started early in the construction industry by pouring concrete with his uncle when he was just sixteen. His next construction job was with a large company, where he started as a carpenter and general laborer and was later promoted to dirt foreman and then bridge foreman. He then accepted the position of bridge superintendent with a new company.

Planning is one of Ray's most important duties as a bridge superintendent. He begins every workday in a meeting with engineers and the project manager to plan the day's work and set individual goals. Ray makes sure that workers are prepared and scheduled so they stay out of each other's way. One of the most difficult aspects of his job is finding and keeping general laborers. The company pays $9 an hour for labor-intensive work such as shoveling dirt or welding metal, while fast-food restaurants competing for the same workers pay $8.

Career Advice. Ray says that he wants to hire people who have a sense of pride and a desire to improve themselves. He also advises young people to stay in high school because a better education will give them more employment opportunities.

Civil Engineers

Civil engineers are road builders. They design and supervise the construction of roads and bridges and spend a lot of time writing reports and consulting with other engineers. Their complex projects often require team effort.

You can typically find office, field, and project engineers on a large road-building job. Office engineers are usually the most junior of the engineers, and the number on each job depends on the amount of redesign work and scheduling needed. Field engineers, as their name implies, work in the field. They are the most immediate support staff for superintendents and are responsible for ensuring that construction continues without a hitch. The project engineer is the head engineer on a road-building job. The entire staff of engineers reports to the project engineer, who reports to the project manager. In addition to managing and scheduling the road-building job, project engineers obtain contracts and ensure that the subcontractors hired by the company complete their work and receive their pay. Subcontractors are hired when another company has greater experience or can perform part of the work at a cheaper rate.

Job Qualifications and Training

A bachelor's degree in engineering is generally required for entry-level engineering jobs. There are about 1,830 institutions in the United States offering programs in engineering that are accredited by the Accreditation Board for Engineering and Technology (ABET). Admissions requirements for undergraduate engineering schools include a solid background in mathematics (algebra, geometry, trigonometry, and calculus); sciences (biology, chemistry, and physics); and courses in social studies, English, humanities, and computers. A typical four-year college curriculum includes a range of courses in the first two years that expose students to mathematics, basic sciences, introductory engineering, humanities, and social sciences. The last two years focus on engineering courses, usually with a concentration in one branch. Although bachelor's degree programs in engineering are designed to be completed in four years, many students take longer to include more electives. Canadian civil engineers can practice as a Professional Engineer after receiving their provincial or territorial license from the regional Association of Professional Engineers.

Beyond formal training, you need to be creative, inquisitive, analytical, and detail oriented to become an engineer. You should also be able to work as part of a team and to communicate well, both orally and in writing. In your first job, you will typically work under the supervision of an experienced engineer, and, depending on the company, you may receive formal classroom or seminar-type training.

Job Outlook and Earnings

Employment opportunities for American or Canadian engineers are expected to increase faster than the average for all occupations. Although a relatively small number of engineers leave the profession each year, many others are promoted to management. As a result, many job openings will stem from replacement needs. Engineers should plan to continue their education throughout their careers because much of their value to an employer depends on their knowledge of the latest technology. By keeping current, engineers are able to provide the best solutions and greatest value to their employers.

The median annual salary of civil engineers is more than $68,000. The middle 50 percent earns between $54,500 and $86,200. The lowest 10 percent earns less than $45,000, and the highest 10 percent earns more than $104,000. The average annual salary for Canadian engineers is CAN$59,600. Engineers with bachelor's degrees receive starting salaries averaging about $48,500 a year, while master's candidates receive about $48,300.

On the Job with a Project Engineer

James William is a project engineer working for a large heavy-construction company. After graduating from college, James worked as an office engineer in Texas for two years, learning the business side of construction. He then returned to school to earn a master's degree in civil engineering that focused on construction management. His master's degree earned James a job in Northern California as an assistant estimator creating bids for work.

His next career move was to a field engineer position in Southern California, where he was soon promoted to project engineer. James was then transferred to Florida as an office and grading engineer for a year before he was promoted to project engineer. In this job, James spent his days wearing a hard hat as he steered a four-wheel-drive pickup around the freeway his company was building. He constantly looked for ways to improve productivity and efficiency, and he spent a lot of time talking to foremen about the building process. Before the highway was finished, James was transferred to a new road-building project in West Virginia. Like James, engineers who build roads move frequently. Sometimes they move before a job is completed, and they always move when a project is finished.

As a project engineer on his new job, James identifies work tasks and creates the master schedule for completing them. He also writes subcontracts and material purchase orders. James solves problems that arise when conflicts occur between new road construction and vehicle traffic on existing roads. In general, James coordinates and facilitates building the project. He reads and interprets construction plans, schedules the work, and helps execute the work plan.

In a typical week, James works anywhere from sixty to seventy hours at the site. Fortunately, his office in a double-wide trailer is parked in the middle of the job site. The long hours can be a downside to working as a project engineer. Other frustrations include frequent delays caused by material shortages and erratic subcontractor schedules as well as frequent weather changes. Still, James enjoys working outside and seeing something actually being built. James aspires to be first a project manager and then an area manager.

Career Advice. James advises anyone interested in construction to be a self-starter and able to handle multiple tasks at one time. He also believes that you will advance faster in your career if you can function well with limited and ambiguous information. Additionally, James points out that being successful in road construction requires the ability to imagine the big picture while focusing on the details.

Project Managers

The ultimate on-site bosses of road-building projects are the project managers. They typically report to an area manager, who then reports to the vice president or president of the construction company.

Project management is a hard-hat job only when project managers visit the site two or more times a day. However, project managers have usually had several hard-hat jobs before being promoted to this position.

Project managers monitor the construction job from a main office in an existing building or in a trailer at the job site. They are on call twenty-four hours a day to deal with delays, bad weather, or emergencies at the site. Their workweeks always include more than forty hours; however, their actual hours depend on the season and the deadlines for completion.

Project managers coordinate and manage people, materials, equipment, budgets, schedules, contracts, and the safety of employees and the general public. They are responsible for selecting and coordinating trade contractors hired to complete specific pieces of the project.

In addition, project managers determine the job's labor requirements and frequently supervise or monitor the hiring and dismissal of workers. Most managers prepare daily reports on the job's progress and requirements for labor, material, machinery, and equipment at the construction site.

To do their jobs effectively, project managers rely heavily on their engineers to organize and run the road-building job on time. They work with the engineers to evaluate various construction methods and determine the most cost-effective plan and schedule. Together, they schedule all required construction site activities into logical, specific steps, budgeting the time required to meet established deadlines.

Job Qualifications and Training

Becoming a project manager requires a solid background in construction, business, and management as well as related work experience in road building. You must be able to read contracts, plans, and specifications, and you should be knowledgeable about construction methods, materials, and regulations. In addition, you will benefit from familiarity with computers and software programs for determining job costs, scheduling, and estimating.

To be a successful project manager, you should be flexible and able to work effectively in a fast-paced environment. You should also be decisive and work well under pressure as you will be bombarded with unexpected occurrences and delays. Being able to coordinate several major activities at once while analyzing and resolving specific problems is essential. You should have good oral and written communications skills and be a strong leader. As a manager, you must establish good working relationships with many different kinds of people, including owners, other managers, engineers, and supervisors.

More than a hundred colleges and universities offer four-year degree programs in construction management. These programs include courses in project control and development, site planning, design, construction methods, construction materials, value analysis, cost estimating, scheduling, contract administration, accounting, business and financial management, building codes and standards, inspection procedures, engineering and architectural sciences, mathematics, statistics, and information technology. Recent graduates from a four-year degree program are typically hired as field or office engineers and then promoted as they gain experience.

About sixty colleges and universities offer a master's degree program in construction management or construction science, and at least two offer a doctorate in the field. Individuals with master's degrees still usually need to gain work experience in construction prior to becoming project managers. They may work as office, field, and project engineers.

Both the American Institute of Constructors (AIC) and the Construction Management Association of America (CMAA) have created voluntary certification programs for construction professionals. To become certified, you must take courses, pass written examinations, and complete verified professional work experience. Although certification is not required to work in the construction industry, voluntary certification can be valuable because it provides evidence of competence and experience.

Job Outlook and Earnings

Employment of project managers is expected to grow as fast as the average for all occupations. You will be more likely to get a job if you have a bachelor's or higher degree in construction management and if you have prior work and supervisory experience. As road-building projects continue to become more complex, the demand for highly trained management personnel will increase.

Earnings for salaried project managers and self-employed construction contractors vary depending upon the size and nature of the construction project, its geographic location, and economic conditions. In addition to typical benefits packages, many project managers receive benefits such as bonuses and use of company cars or trucks.

The median annual earnings of project managers are about $73,700. The middle 50 percent earns between $56,000 and $98,300. The lowest 10 percent earns less than $43,200, while the highest 10 percent earns more than $135,700. Canadian project managers can expect to receive an average annual salary of about CAN$60,000.

On the Job with a Project Manager

Jim Rose is the project manager on a $55 million highway and bridge construction job in North Carolina. He is responsible for everything that happens on the job. For a job this size to be successful, Jim needs a strong support staff to complete paperwork and scheduling for his approval.

One of Jim's primary concerns is on-the-job safety. As a result, he drives through the work site at least twice daily to check on safety and job progress. Jim typically works fifty to sixty hours per week and tries to schedule his staff so that no one person is over-worked. He also helps his superintendents and foremen set and meet goals.

Jim attended a community college for two years and then trans-ferred to a four-year college to earn a degree in civil engineering. He started in the construction industry as a surveyor for a small company, gaining valuable exposure to all areas of work in the field. Because it was a small company, he was frequently asked to step in and help, doing whatever was needed. Jim next moved up to office engineer, and then he became a project engineer. When a larger firm bought the company, Jim became a project manager. Jim says working in heavy construction has fulfilled his boyhood ambition to build things, but he also enjoys meeting so many peo-ple with such different backgrounds.

Career Advice. For a career in building roads, Jim recommends that you earn a degree in civil engineering or construction man-agement and find a company to intern with during your college summers.

On the Job with a Company President
Today, Dan Beaty is president of a small family-owned bridge and highway construction company that averages between eighty and one hundred employees. He started in high school, however, working summer vacations on highway bridge repair projects as a construction laborer. Wearing a hard hat at all times, he operated a jackhammer to demolish the existing concrete structure; drove piling for support of the new bridge; erected new structural steel; poured new concrete footings, decks, and piers; and excavated and compacted soil for a new roadway. Dan continued these basic laborer activities for the same construction company until he graduated from college with a degree in civil engineering.

After graduating, Dan took on basic surveying and layout duties for typical bridge jobs. He also estimated and managed labor and equipment crews. This involved spending about half of his time in the field to help the superintendent direct crews (a hard-hat job). He spent the other half in the office arranging and scheduling activities and deliveries of materials on a specific job. As his experience grew, Dan assumed responsibility for multiple projects, acting as a senior project manager. He directed other managers who were overseeing specific projects. His time on the job site was reduced to a few hours a week to meet with project managers and review schedules, project safety, and assign equipment. Although Dan is now president of the company, the size of the company also requires him to act as senior project manager. He still spends 10 to 15 percent of his time in the field wearing a hard hat.

A Day on the Job. While Dan must be able to multitask and be flexible in his daily routine, a typical day on the job in his position entails the following tasks:

- meet with estimators and discuss new projects to estimate
- review estimates (production rates), assess risk, assign profit markup, and communicate to the estimator
- meet with project managers and discuss issues and schedules
- review project safety inspections and follow up on any issues raised
- review bills and sign checks
- meet with equipment vendors regarding new purchases
- review job cost reports and equipment utilization
- talk with clients (potential and existing)

Climbing the Career Path. Dan's advice for a successful career as a civil engineer is to start with a strong summer internship or co-op program with a construction or engineering firm. To make management positions within many companies, a degree in either civil engineering or construction technology is highly recommended. A few years as a project engineer or junior estimator is an excellent way to learn the details of a job while understanding all the costs involved in a complete project. Site superintendent or project manager is another important position that provides you the opportunity to expand your knowledge of the business along with beginning to manage people. As your career grows, you will gain responsibility for larger projects, multiple projects, or additional estimators as a senior project manager or senior estimator. Depending on the size of the company you may then have opportunities to manage a specific division as the division vice president.

Safety Workers

Most large construction companies have one or more people in charge of safety training and enforcement on each job site. On some jobs, safety workers help with the hands-on building process, while on others the sole responsibility is safety. They conduct weekly meetings with the entire staff to ensure that everyone is aware of company safety standards. Safety workers also train all of the new employees so they understand the company's safety policies.

When accidents occur, safety workers are the first people on the scene. Their training in first aid and CPR helps them handle the kinds of accidents that occur in building roads. After an incident, safety workers file accident reports.

For More Information

For information about jobs as general laborers, contact local road-building companies and the local office of your state's employment service.

General information about the work of construction equipment operators is available from:

Construction Sector Council
220 Laurier Avenue West, Suite 1150
Ottawa, ON K1P 5Z9
Canada
www.careersinconstruction.ca

National Center for Construction Education and Research
University of Florida
3600 NW Forty-Third Street, Building G
Gainesville, FL 32606
www.nccer.org

For information about apprenticeships or work opportunities for equipment operators, contact a local chapter of the International Union of Operating Engineers, a local or state apprenticeship agency, or your state employment service.

High school students can learn more about a career in civil engineering by contacting the Junior Engineering Technical Society (JETS) at:

JETS-Guidance
1420 King Street, Suite 405
Alexandria, VA 22314
www.jets.org

To learn about accredited engineering programs, contact:

The Accreditation Board for Engineering and Technology, Inc.
111 Market Place, Suite 1050
Baltimore, MD 21202
www.abet.org

Canadian Council of Professional Engineers
180 Elgin Street, Suite 1100
Ottawa, ON K2P 2K3
Canada
www.engineerscanada.ca

Information is available on accredited construction science and management programs from:

American Council for Construction Education
1717 North Loop 1604 East, Suite 320
San Antonio, TX 78232
www.acce-hq.org

CHAPTER THREE

Constructing Houses and Other Buildings

Every day 8.3 million people are helping construct buildings in the United States. More than two million houses and other buildings are being built every year. It is estimated that the construction industry will need an additional 1.1 million workers by 2012 to meet demand as new buildings are built and older building are renovated.

Constructing buildings is one of the largest industries in the United States and Canada. Think of all the new factories, shopping malls, office buildings, schools, apartment houses, and homes under construction throughout the country. Think also of all the additions, alterations, and repairs that are being done to buildings. All of this construction adds up to hundreds of billions of dollars each year and to an immense number of jobs for hard-hat workers. In fact, more than 150 careers are involved in the construction of a building.

Construction Workers

It takes workers from many career fields to construct buildings. Most of these are skilled crafts workers, apprentices, and laborers. Their occupations include:

- air-conditioning installers
- bricklayers

- carpenters
- concrete masons
- drywall installers
- electricians
- floor workers
- glaziers
- heating workers
- insulation installers
- ironworkers
- painters
- pipe fitters
- plasterers
- plumbers
- roofers
- sheet metal workers
- steamfitters
- stonemasons

The construction of buildings also requires several layers of management. Generally, the larger the project, the more levels of management it needs. In most building projects, subcontractors are hired to handle specific jobs such as carpentry, plumbing, or electrical work. Their work is coordinated by the company selected as general contractor of the job. Like the subcontractors, the general contractor may have a small, medium, or large firm.

On a small project, the owner of the company may act as general contractor, completing most jobs while hiring one or more subcontractors to do specific work. As projects get larger, the general contractor will place a construction manager in charge of overseeing all aspects of the project until it is completed. The construction manager will be assisted by superintendents who oversee the work of the foremen. They, in turn, directly oversee the work of the crafts workers, apprentices, and laborers to make sure their jobs are well done.

Work Hazards and Conditions

Constructing buildings can be hazardous work. Many of the necessary tools—such as nail guns, saws, drills, and welding equipment—are potentially dangerous. Job sites are often cluttered with all kinds of building materials that can trip workers. Because much of this work is performed on ladders, scaffolding, and in other high places, there is a real danger of serious falls or of objects falling on workers. Unfortunately, the incidence of work-related injuries in construction is higher than for most other careers. Employers increasingly emphasize safety, and many government regulations now ensure safer workplaces. If you choose a career constructing buildings, you will usually wear a hard hat on the job.

Safety measures help make construction less dangerous, but the work can be unpleasant for other reasons. You will work outside or in partially enclosed structures during downpours and heat waves, and you'll be exposed to considerable noise from the tools and machinery. You may frequently have to bend, stoop, kneel, and lift heavy materials. At times, working in cramped quarters can make it difficult to complete tasks. You can also expect to work more than a typical forty-hour workweek and to work some evenings, weekends, and holidays to get jobs done on time.

If you choose to construct buildings, you will probably work for a small company. Eight out of ten construction companies have fewer than ten employees. Your best opportunities for employment are in highly populated areas that are growing rapidly.

From the Ground Up: The Building Construction Career Path

If you enter one of the many crafts involved in constructing buildings, you could advance from being an entry-level laborer to the owner of a company. The bottom rung on the construction craft ladder is that of helper or laborer who performs unskilled physical labor. At the same time, you would learn the skills that crafts workers need and could work your way into a position as a a journey-level crafts worker.

Instead of following the on-the-job route, many young people try to advance more rapidly by enrolling in apprenticeship programs sponsored by unions, trade associations, and employers. Even more rapid advancement may be possible for those who go through community and technical college programs.

After several years as a skilled crafts worker, you could advance to a position as foreman and then, with additional experience, to superintendent. Once you have become a skilled crafts worker, you can start your own business with only a moderate financial outlay. Whatever route you take, all of these jobs require hard hats when you work on commercial projects.

The route up the career ladder is different for college graduates with degrees in construction management. They usually work for larger contractors and start as management trainees or construction manager assistants. Engineering graduates may start as field engineers. Both can ultimately advance to construction managers or even to owners of their own general contracting firms.

On the Job with a Construction Company Owner

Grafton Brandt began his career in construction right after graduating from high school. He followed his older brother into this career and started out as a concrete mason pouring driveways. After six months as a mason, he enlisted in the Marine Corps and served for three years. After leaving the service, Grafton found work as a laborer for a company building large family homes. Over the next eight years, he earned several promotions until he eventually became the company's youngest-ever production manager.

With this level of experience under his belt, Grafton left the company to work as a vice president for a firm that built town-houses. He next moved to another company where, as vice president, he oversaw the building of single-family homes. Today, Grafton and his family have started their own company, which builds single-family homes. His firm operates as subcontractor to another firm with an already-solid reputation.

As president of the family-owned company, Grafton looks for land to purchase and for investors. He also oversees all of the subcontractors hired to help with building homes. The most challenging part of his job is hiring competent people, and his greatest reward comes from the knowledge that he is creating homes for people. He takes tremendous pride in doing his job well and thereby making the home owners happy. Grafton's ascent up the career ladder from laborer to president of his family's company shows that real opportunities exist for hard-hat wearers to own a construction business.

Career Advice. Grafton says that constructing buildings demands the desire to work hard and the ability to feel a sense of achievement for a job done well.

Bricklayers and Stonemasons

Bricklaying and stonemasonry are two common crafts in the construction business. These similar crafts help in the construction of walkways, freeways, building walls and exteriors, fireplaces, and chimneys by creating attractive, durable surfaces and structures. The work of bricklayers (also called brick masons) is everywhere—from simple pathways to ornate exteriors on high-rise buildings. Bricklayers use brick, of course, but they also work with precast masonry panels, concrete block, and other masonry materials. Stonemasons build stone walls and set stone exteriors and floors, usually for nonresidential structures such as churches, hotels, and office buildings. Most of their projects use natural cut stones such as marble, granite, and limestone, but they also work with artificial stones made from concrete, marble chips, and other masonry materials.

The Bricklayer's Job

Bricklayers spread mortar—a mixture of cement, sand, and water—as a bed for the bricks. Then they either cut bricks with a hammer and chisel or saw them to fit around windows, doors, and other openings. Finally, they use jointing tools to fill mortar joints for a sealed, neat, and uniform appearance. If you are new to the field of brick masonry, you will begin in the position of hod carrier, or helper, assisting bricklayers by mixing mortar, setting up scaffolding, and bringing bricks and other materials to them.

In the past, bricklayers who worked on nonresidential interiors primarily built block partition walls and elevator shafts. Now, they perform more versatile work with many materials. For example, bricklayers install lightweight insulated panels used in skyscraper construction.

The Stonemason's Job

If you become a stonemason, you may find yourself working from a set of drawings in which each stone has been numbered for identification. Helpers locate and carry these prenumbered stones to you, and a derrick operator using a hoist lifts the larger stone pieces into place, if necessary. When building a stone wall, masons set the first course of stones into a shallow bed of mortar, align them with wedges, and position them with a hard rubber mallet. As the wall progresses, masons remove the wedges, fill the joints, and smooth the mortar to provide an attractive finish. Masons use a special hammer and chisel to cut stone along the grain to create various shapes and sizes. The more valuable pieces of stone are often cut with a saw fitted with a diamond blade.

Job Qualifications and Training

Bricklayers and stonemasons pick up most of their skills informally by observing and learning from experienced workers. If you enter either field with few or no skills, you will begin as a helper, laborer, or mason tender and will carry materials, move scaffolds, and mix mortar. Experienced workers will show you how to spread mortar, lay brick and block, and set stone. You can also receive training in vocational education schools, but the best way to learn the necessary skills is through a three-year apprenticeship program that combines on-the-job training with 144 hours of classroom instruction. Subjects include blueprint reading, mathematics, layout work, and sketching. You must be at least seventeen years old and in good physical condition to apply to be an apprentice. A high school education is preferred, and courses in mathematics, mechanical drawing, and shop are also helpful.

Job Outlook and Earnings

More than 182,000 bricklayers and stonemasons work throughout the United States and over 13,000 in Canada. Almost three out of every ten are self-employed and specialize in small jobs. Job prospects for skilled bricklayers and stonemasons in the United States and Canada are very good. Population growth and new businesses will create a need for new houses, factories, schools, hospitals, offices, and other structures, increasing the need for bricklayers and stonemasons. In addition, the need to repair and restore old masonry buildings will increase. However, like employment for virtually all other construction workers, employment of bricklayers and stonemasons is sensitive to changes in the economy. When the level of construction drops, so does the level of employment.

Bricklayers and stonemasons receive an hourly wage. Earnings can be reduced at times due to poor weather, delays caused by waiting for other workers to finish their jobs, and downturns in construction activity. Median hourly earnings for bricklayers are about $21 and stonemasons are about $17. The middle 50 percent in these two trades earns between $13 and $26. The lowest 10 percent earns just over $10, and the highest 10 percent earns more than $28. In Canada, bricklayers and stonemasons earn a median hourly wage of about CAN$22. The lowest rate is about CAN$17, with the highest rate being over CAN$23. In general, apprentices or helpers start at about 50 percent of the wage rate paid to experienced workers.

Carpenters

Duties for carpenters often vary depending on where they are employed. Some carpenters who are self-employed or work for small contractors perform every aspect of the job, while those who work for specialty trade contractors specialize in just one or two activities, such as making forms for concrete construction, erecting scaffolding, or completing the finishing work. Although carpentry jobs can be quite varied, most involve the same basic steps. Carpenters work from blueprints or instructions from supervisors to accomplish the layout—measuring, marking, and arranging materials. They then cut and shape wood, plastic, fiberglass, or drywall, using hand and power tools such as chisels, planes, saws, drills, and sanders. Next, they join the materials together with nails, screws, staples, or adhesives. The final step is to check the accuracy of their work with levels, rules, plumb bobs, and framing squares and make any necessary adjustments. At times, carpenters' jobs can be fairly easy, such as when they work with prefabricated components—stairs or wall panels, for example—that can be installed in a single operation.

Job Qualifications and Training

Prospective carpenters should complete high school and have taken courses in carpentry, shop, mechanical drawing, and general mathematics. They need the ability to solve arithmetic problems quickly and accurately because carpentry involves a lot of math—especially for measuring. Other important skills for carpenters are hand-eye coordination, physical fitness, and a good sense of balance.

Most carpenters learn the trade through on-the-job training, informally picking up their skills by working under the supervision of experienced workers. They can also enroll in good vocational programs to help them learn carpentry skills. Employers, however, often recommend apprenticeship programs that combine on-the-job training with related classroom instruction.

As an apprentice, you will learn elementary structural design and become familiar with common carpentry jobs, such as layout, form building, rough framing, and outside and inside finishing. You will also learn how to use the tools, machines, equipment, and materials of the trade. Classroom instruction covers safety, first aid, blueprint reading, freehand sketching, basic mathematics, and different carpentry techniques.

Canadian carpenters must obtain training and experience similar to those in the United States. In addition, qualified carpenters can obtain an interprovincial (Red Seal) trade certificate, which allows Canadian carpenters to work throughout the country.

On-the-job training is not as thorough as apprenticeships because the degree of training and supervision you receive depends on the size of your firm. For example, a small contractor specializing in home building may only provide training in rough framing.

Job Outlook and Earnings

Job opportunities for carpenters are plentiful because a high turnover rate creates a constant need to replace existing workers. Many leave each year to transfer to other careers or to retire. The total number of job openings for carpenters is usually greater than for other craft occupations because so many carpenters are needed in building construction.

Prospective carpenters should realize that they will likely experience periods of unemployment because of the short-term nature of many construction projects and the ups and downs of the construction industry. Interest rates, the availability of mortgage funds, government spending, and business investment affect how much construction is under way. The better the economy is, the more job openings there are for carpenters.

The median hourly wage for carpenters is about $17.50. The middle 50 percent earns between $13.50 and $24. The lowest 10 percent earns less than $11, and the highest 10 percent earns more than $30 per hour. Carpenters working in residential building earn less than those working on commercial construction projects. All carpenters can lose earnings because of bad weather.

On the Job with a Carpenter

Greg Abbott's father was a carpenter who specialized in finishing work. After graduating from high school and working odd jobs for a year, Greg decided to follow in his father's footsteps and become a carpenter. He even decided to work at the same company, which built three-story condominiums. To work there, he had to join a union and enter its four-year apprenticeship program. On his first job, he worked side by side with his father as they did trim work on the condominiums. As he continued his apprenticeship, Greg rotated jobs to learn such carpentry skills as framing, siding, and installing windows.

When construction slowed for Greg's first employer, he went to work crafting exterior trim for another company. In fact, he switched companies several times as work slowed or closed down before he landed work at a precast concrete company. In this job, he built forms for concrete molds that would be used to create panels. Greg points with pride to the fact that these panels were used in the construction of several prominent buildings in the San Francisco area.

Carpenters can advance to become carpentry supervisors, which is exactly what Greg accomplished on his next job working for a company that built expensive homes. He supervised a crew of ten carpenters who had the task of making sure each house was ready for the plumbers, electricians, and heating and air-conditioning installers.

When work slowed, Greg began supplementing his income with contracting work on the side. When he had more outside work than carpentry work, Greg decided to become an independent contractor.

Becoming a Contractor. Today, Greg owns a company that specializes in renovating and modernizing homes, including building entire additions. Besides carpentry, Greg also handles the electrical and plumbing work. He is able to take on these extra tasks because he holds a general contractor's license. Greg usually works alone, but he hires a helper at times and subcontractors for special work such as laying floors, roofing, and pouring concrete.

To become a successful contractor, Greg had to know the nature and quantity of materials needed to properly complete a job. He also had to estimate with accuracy a job's cost and how long it should take to complete. While Greg is working on one job, he must look ahead by soliciting new jobs as well as obtaining building permits. Being a contractor requires the ability to juggle several tasks at once. The success of his company demonstrates that Greg has this skill.

Cement Masons

Concrete is one of the most common and durable materials used in construction. Once set, concrete—a mixture of Portland cement, sand, gravel, and water—becomes the foundation for everything from decorative patios and floors to huge dams. If you become a concrete mason, you will place and finish the concrete. You might add color to the surface, expose small stones in concrete walls and sidewalks, or fabricate concrete beams, columns, and panels.

The first step in placing concrete is to prepare the site by setting forms for holding the concrete to the desired angle and depth. Next, you use shovels or special tools to spread the concrete. You then guide a straightedge back and forth across the top of the forms to level the concrete. Right after leveling the surface, you smooth it with a long-handled tool called a bull float.

After the concrete has been leveled and floated, you or a concrete finisher complete the process by pressing an edger between the forms and the concrete and guiding it along the edge and the surface. This process produces slightly rounded edges and helps prevent chipping or cracking. A tool called a groover is used to make joints or grooves at specific intervals that also help control cracking.

The final step is to trowel the surface using either a powered or a hand trowel to create a smooth finish. For a coarse, nonskid finish, you brush the surface with a broom or stiff-bristled brush. For a pebble finish, you spray the surface with a chemical retardant, then wash and brush away the top layer to expose the small aggregate gravel mixed into the concrete.

On concrete surfaces that will remain exposed after the forms are stripped, such as columns, ceilings, and wall panels, you cut away high spots with a hammer and chisel. Next, you fill any large indentations with a cement paste and smooth the surface with a rubbing Carborundum stone. Finally, you coat the exposed area with a rich cement mixture by using either a special tool or a coarse cloth to rub the concrete into a uniform finish.

Throughout the entire process, cement masons must monitor how the wind, heat, or cold is affecting the curing of the concrete. This requires a thorough knowledge of concrete; good masons can determine what is happening to the concrete simply by sight or touch and take measures to prevent defects.

Job Qualifications and Training

A successful cement mason needs to enjoy demanding jobs and be able to work without close supervision. Most employers prefer high school graduates who are at least eighteen years old and in good physical condition because cement work is fast paced and strenuous, and it requires continuous physical effort. High school courses in general science, shop, mathematics, blueprint reading, or mechanical drawing provide a helpful background. You must also have the ability to get along with others because you will frequently work in teams.

Cement masons and concrete finishers learn the craft in the same way as bricklayers, stonemasons, and carpenters learn theirs—through on-the-job training as helpers, by attending trade or technical schools, or by participating in three-year apprenticeship programs. On-the-job training programs consist of informal instruction from experienced workers. You begin with tasks such as edging, jointing, and using a straightedge on freshly placed concrete. As your experience grows, your assignments become more complex, and you should be able to tackle more difficult finishing work within a short time.

Job Outlook and Earnings

Employment growth and job prospects for cement masons in the United States and Canada are expected to be good and grow at about the average rate for all jobs. However, opportunities for skilled masons are expected to be excellent as the demand for these workers will exceed the supply needed to build all the factories, office buildings, hotels, shopping centers, schools, hospitals, homes, and other structures planned for the next few years. Like employment levels for other careers in construction, the employment level of cement masons is directly related to the economy.

The median hourly wage of cement masons and concrete finishers is nearly $16. The middle 50 percent earns between $12 and $21. The lowest 10 percent earns about $10, while the highest 10 percent earns more than $27. In Canada, concrete masons earn an average CAN$19.67 with the highest rate being about CAN$23 per hour.

On the Job with a Cement Mason

When he was just eight years old, Chris Beckwith started shadowing his cement-mason father on job sites. These early experiences convinced him that cement masonry was the career path that he wanted to follow. In fact, Chris was so eager to get started that he completed high school early. Then, at nearly eighteen, he was able to join the cement mason's union because the company where his father worked needed employees.

For more than thirteen years, Chris worked for the same company, which involved only commercial work. Chris started in an entry-level job. He dug ditches and served as a gofer, which means that he would go for the tools and materials the cement masons needed. At the same time, he watched the masons work and began learning procedures by giving them a hand. To learn more about the job, Chris enrolled in a three-year union apprenticeship program, attending eight hours of classes every Saturday for nine months of the year. The classes taught him the basics, and the job let him see how they worked.

After Chris worked as a crew member for several years, he became a crew leader, helping the foreman direct a crew of as many as twelve workers. He also acted as foreman when needed. His next step up the career ladder as foreman involved both supervising an experienced crew and training new workers.

Cement masons and other crafts workers must buy their own tools. Chris bought so many that he only had to buy a truck and pass the state contractor's license examination when he started his own company from his home six years ago. He started with only one laborer besides himself, and business slowly increased. Now, Chris works alongside four employees and will soon hire a foreman to replace him on the job site so he can devote more time to looking for work for his company. At first, Chris's company only performed plain work. However, Chris enjoys expanding his skills, so he learned cement stamping and staining at seminars and now provides fancy work for his customers.

Career Advice. Chris wants future cement masons to realize that they need patience because it takes time to master the skills of this craft. He believes that you will know the basics after three years, reach crafts worker level after six years, and be ready to start your own company after ten.

Electricians

Electricity is essential in our everyday lives for lighting, power, air-conditioning, refrigeration, and many of the gadgets we use. Electricians are the hard-hat workers who install, connect, test, and maintain electrical systems for a variety of purposes, including climate control, security, and communications.

Electricians work with blueprints to install electrical systems in structures such as factories, office buildings, and homes. Blueprints are plans that show the location of circuits, outlets, load centers, panel boards, and other equipment.

If you work inside factories and offices, your first step as an electrician is to place conduit (pipe or tubing) inside partitions, walls, or other concealed areas. You then fasten small metal or plastic boxes to walls that store electrical switches and outlets. Next, you pull insulated wires or cables through the conduit to complete circuits between the boxes.

In residential construction, you use plastic-covered wire instead of conduit. Your next task is to connect the wire to circuit breakers, transformers, or other components. Electricians make the connection by twisting the ends of the wire together with pliers and covering the ends with special plastic connectors. If stronger connections are required, they may use an electric soldering iron to melt metal onto the twisted wires and then cover them with durable electrical tape.

After completing a wiring job, electricians use testing equipment, such as ohmmeters, voltmeters, and oscilloscopes, to check the circuits for proper connections.

As an electrician, you could also use your skills to install coaxial or fiber-optic cable for computers and other telecommunications equipment. It is becoming more common for electricians to install telephone, computer wiring and equipment, and fire alarm and security systems. Another aspect of your job could be maintenance work, especially in factories.

To work safely in this trade, you need to wear a hard hat and follow safety procedures at all times. Electricians risk serious injury from electrical shock, falls, and cuts every day on the job.

Job Qualifications and Training

To become an electrician, you should have a high school diploma and have taken courses in mathematics, electricity, electronics, mechanical drawing, science, and shop. A background in electronics is becoming increasingly important because of the growing use of complex electronic controls on manufacturing equipment. Other prerequisites for this career include average physical strength, agility, and good color vision because you frequently have to identify wires by their color.

Most electricians enter this trade after completing a four- or five-year apprenticeship program, although some still learn their skills informally on the job. Apprenticeship programs include at least 144 hours of classroom and about 2,000 hours of on-the-job training. The classroom part of the apprenticeship program teaches blueprint reading, electrical theory, electronics, mathematics, electrical code requirements, and safety and first aid practices. It also includes specialized training in welding, communications, fire-alarm systems, and cranes and elevators.

Canadian electricians also complete a four- to five-year apprenticeship program. In addition, trade certification is compulsory in all provinces and territories. Electricians may also get the interprovincial (Red Seal) trade certification in order to work throughout the country.

Job Outlook and Earnings

Job opportunities are expected to be very good for skilled electricians because a smaller number of workers are entering training programs. The demand for electricians will be stimulated by new construction and existing maintenance work and by new technologies, including the installation of robots and automated manufacturing in factories.

Depending on their experience, apprentices usually start out earning between 30 and 50 percent of the rate paid to experienced electricians. The median hourly wage of electricians is nearly $21. The middle 50 percent earns between $16 and $28. The lowest 10 percent earns less than $12, and the highest 10 percent earns more than $35.

Plumbers and Pipe Fitters

You may be familiar with plumbers who come to your home to unclog a drain or install an appliance, but plumbers and pipe fitters also install, maintain, and repair many different types of pipe systems. If you become a plumber you will install and repair the water, waste disposal, drainage, and gas systems in homes and commercial and industrial buildings. You will also install plumbing fixtures—bathtubs, showers, sinks, and toilets—and appliances such as dishwashers and water heaters. If you become a pipe fitter, you will install and repair both high- and low-pressure pipe systems used in manufacturing, in the generation of electricity, and in heating and cooling buildings. You will also install automatic controls that are used to regulate those systems. In either job, you will frequently work in uncomfortable or cramped positions and will need to wear a hard hat to protect your head.

Depending on the type of project, plumbers use a wide variety of materials and construction techniques. Residential water systems use copper, steel, and plastic pipe that can be installed by one or two workers. Municipal sewer systems are made of large cast-iron pipes, and their installation normally requires crews of pipe fitters.

When plumbers install piping at a site, they work from blueprints or drawings that show the planned location of pipes, plumbing fixtures, and appliances. First, they lay out the job to fit the piping into the structure with the least waste of material possible. Then, they measure and mark areas where pipes will be installed and connected. Sometimes, they have to cut holes in the walls, ceilings, and floors. And, for some systems, plumbers may have to hang steel supports from ceiling joists to hold the pipe in place.

To assemble a system, they use saws, pipe cutters, and pipe-bending machines. They connect lengths of pipe with fittings appropriate to the material used; for example, they use adhesives to connect the sections and fittings of plastic pipe. Finally, they check to make sure their connections are secure by using pressure gauges to test for water flow and leaks.

Job Qualifications and Training

Virtually all plumbers and pipe fitters have finished some type of apprenticeship training that lasts from four to five years and combines on-the-job training with classes. Classroom subjects include drafting and blueprint reading, mathematics, applied physics and chemistry, safety, and local plumbing codes and regulations. On the job, apprentices first learn basic skills, such as identifying grades and types of pipe, using the tools of the trade, and safely unloading materials. Although there are no uniform national licensing requirements for plumbers, most communities require them to be licensed. Canada requires plumbers and pipe fitters to hold trade certification in all provinces and territories except Newfoundland, Manitoba, Northwest Territories, and the Yukon. Interprovincial trade certification is available for those people who want to work throughout the country.

Job Outlook and Earnings

Opportunities for skilled plumbers and pipe fitters are expected to be excellent as growth in demand outpaces the supply of workers being trained. Workers with welding experience will have the best opportunities. Because construction projects provide only temporary employment, both plumbers and pipe fitters may experience bouts of unemployment. Job openings will vary from area to area depending on the construction activity and economic conditions.

Plumbers and pipe fitters earn a median hourly wage of about $20.50. The middle 50 percent of all plumbers and pipe fitters earns between $15 and $28. The lowest 10 percent earns about $12.30, and the highest 10 percent earns more than $34. Apprentices usually begin with an hourly rate about half of the rate paid to experienced plumbers and pipe fitters.

On the Job with a Plumber

After high school, Anthony Jacobs found a job with a plumbing company that serviced both residential and commercial plumbing jobs. His first job was to deliver tubs, toilets, washbasins, and other supplies and materials to sites where the company worked. This convinced Anthony that he would like to become a plumber.

While it can be difficult to enter union apprenticeship programs, Anthony's company was willing to sponsor him. He also had to pass a test that showed he possessed the necessary skills to become a plumber. Anthony started his six-year apprenticeship by fitting pipe in residences. He also worked on a school remodeling project, removing asbestos and installing new boilers and a science laboratory. He quickly learned that plumbers tackle a variety of jobs.

Anthony points out that there is a difference between residential and commercial plumbing work. In residential work, the pace is faster and you almost always work alone. However, in commercial work you frequently have a helper to lift heavy pipes and materials. Another difference is that commercial plumbers always wear a hard hat on the job, but residential plumbers may not.

Structural and Reinforcing Metalworkers

If you become a structural or reinforcing metalworker, you will help build large offices, skyscrapers, and power transmission towers that have frames made of steel columns, beams, and girders and of concrete reinforced with steel bars or wire fabric. Within the buildings, you will create stairways, catwalks, floor gratings, ladders, window frames, and railings.

When you work high in the air, you need to reduce the risk of injury by using safety devices, such as safety belts, scaffolding, and nets. And, of course, you will always wear a hard hat to protect your head.

Before construction begins, metalworkers must erect steel frames and assemble the cranes and derricks that move structural steel, reinforcing bars, buckets of concrete, lumber, and other materials and equipment around the construction site.

The structural metal arrives at the site in sections. Then it is lifted into position by a crane, and the metalworkers connect the sections.

It is the job of structural metalworkers to connect the steel columns, beams, and girders according to the blueprints. One metalworker directs the hoist operator while another holds a rope to keep the steel from swinging as it is hoisted up in the air and placed in the framework. Then, several workers position the steel to align with the holes in the framework and bolt or weld the piece permanently in place.

The reinforcing metalworkers have a different job. They follow the blueprints to set the bars in the forms that hold concrete. They fasten the bars together by tying wire around them with pliers. When reinforcing floors, the workers place blocks under the bars to hold them in the air. Occasionally, they have to cut bars with metal shears or torches, bend them by hand or machine, or weld them with arc-welding equipment.

Job Qualifications and Training

Metalworkers need to be agile and have good balance, eyesight, and depth perception because they may work on narrow beams and girders at great heights. Obviously, they should not be afraid of heights or suffer from dizziness.

The best way to learn how to be a metalworker is through a three- or four-year apprenticeship that combines on-the-job experience with class work. Only a few workers enter this trade without an apprenticeship, and they may have participated in an extensive training program offered by a contractor.

Canadian metalworkers are required to receive trade certification in most provinces and territories. Interprovincial certification (Red Seal) is available for those workers who want to work throughout the country.

Job Outlook and Earnings

The United States and Canada expect average job growth for opportunities for metalworkers. Workers who are willing to relocate will have greater opportunities for employment. Most openings in this field will result from the need to replace experienced metalworkers who transfer to other occupations or retire.

The number of job openings for metalworkers will fluctuate from year to year as economic conditions and the level of construction activity change. Metalworkers are among those most likely to be put out of work when downturns in the economy slow new construction. Metalworkers earn an average hourly wage of $18.50. The middle 50 percent earn between $13 and $27. The lowest 10 percent earns $10, while the highest 10 percent earns over $34 per hour. Metalworkers who are union members typically have slightly higher hourly earnings.

For More Information

For in-depth information about the careers described in this chapter, pick up the following books:

Rowh, Mark. *Opportunities in Metalworking Careers*. New York: McGraw-Hill, 2008.

Sheldon, Roger. *Opportunities in Carpentry Careers*. New York: McGraw-Hill, 2007.

Sumichrast, Michael. *Opportunities in Building Construction Careers*. New York: McGraw-Hill, 2007.

For information about apprenticeships and work opportunities in the construction of buildings, contact local contractors, trade unions, or the nearest office of your state employment service or state apprenticeship agency. For more information about individual trades, contact:

The Brick Industry Association
1850 Centennial Park Drive, Suite 301
Reston, VA 20191
www.bia.org

Canadian Home Builders' Association
150 Laurier Avenue West, Suite 500
Ottawa, ON K1P 5J4
Canada
www.chba.ca

Canadian Masonry Contractors' Association
360 Superior Boulevard
Mississauga, ON L5T 2N7
Canada
www.canadamasonrycentre.com/cmca

Home Builders Institute of America
1201 Fifteenth Street NW, Sixth Floor
Washington, DC 20005
www.hbi.org

Independent Electrical Contractors
4401 Ford Avenue, Suite 1100
Alexandria, VA 22302
www.ieci.org

International Brotherhood of Electrical Workers Canada
1450 Meyerside Drive, Suite 300
Mississauga, ON L5T 2N5
Canada
www.ibew1st.org

Plumbing-Heating-Cooling Contractors Association
180 South Washington Street
PO Box 6808
Falls Church, VA 22046
www.phccweb.org

Portland Cement Association
5420 Old Orchard Road
Skokie, IL 60077
www.cement.org

CHAPTER FOUR

Jobs in the Mining Industry

G old! The word led to thousands of people rushing to California in the mid-1800s with dreams of striking it rich. Mining gold and the wealth of other natural resources in the United States has played an important part in the country's development. The cities of Pittsburgh, Gary, and Duluth owe their early development largely to coal mines. And the gold rush to California helped lead to the development of the West. By the start of the twentieth century, mining had become a major industry in the United States. Minerals now mined in the United States include coal, copper, iron, gold, silver, uranium, lead, zinc, and bauxite—from which aluminum is extracted—as well as stone, sand, gravel, and clay.

If you choose a career in mining, you will wear a hard hat on the job unless you work in an office. Still, whenever you leave the office to visit a mine site, you will have to put on a hard hat.

A Variety of Mining Methods

Mining is the process of taking minerals from the earth. The methods used depend on whether the deposits lie on the surface or far underground. Most mines are highly mechanized operations, except those operated by a single miner or just a few.

Surface Mining

Miners who remove mineral deposits at or near the surface of the earth will find jobs that involve the following methods:

- **Dredging.** Heavy minerals such as gold and tin are mined from gravel and mineral-bearing layers by using a large machine called a dredge that floats on a pond. Material is scooped up by a chain of buckets and deposited on the dredge for washing, sorting, and collecting the valuable minerals.
- **Open-pit mining.** Most iron and copper ores come from open-pit mines. First, waste materials are removed from the surface. Next, explosives are used to break up the mineral-bearing rocks. This material is excavated from the surface in horizontal layers and carried out of the oval- or bowl-shaped pits by trucks or trains.
- **Strip mining.** Machines or explosives are used to break up coal or other ore lying on the surface. It is then loaded on trucks or railroad cars. These mines generally have the appearance of a wide, shallow, flat-bottom pit.
- **Quarrying.** Quarries typically have steep faces. The minerals may be drilled or blasted with explosives or simply shoveled from the ground. Limestone, gypsum, sand, and gravel are mined from quarries.

Underground Mining

You can find underground mines beneath any type of surface and in any location—even under cities. These mines can be thousands of feet deep and have many tunnels. Three basic methods are used in underground mining:

- **Conventional mining.** This is the oldest method and requires the most workers. It involves drilling holes, placing explosives, and blasting. After the blast, the material is scooped up and carried to the surface.

- **Continuous mining.** Drilling and blasting are eliminated with this method. A continuous-mining machine cuts and rips out the minerals and loads them directly into a conveyor or shuttle car for transport to the surface.
- **Longwall mining.** In this method, just like the continuous-mining method, large machines are used to remove the ore and load it onto a conveyor; the difference is that hydraulic jacks are used to reinforce the roof of the tunnel.

Work Hazards and Conditions

Working conditions in surface and underground mines are quite challenging and frequently dangerous. If you choose to work above ground, you will be exposed to all kinds of weather. You will also work close to or operate noisy excavating machinery, trucks, conveyors, and shuttle cars. There may be additional noise and vibrations from blasting. The work site is likely to be dusty and may contain pollutants and dangerous waste deposits, so you will need to take special precautions to protect yourself from these hazards.

In an underground mine, you trade natural light for electric lighting, and, in some areas, you must rely solely on the illumination from your hard hat. Fresh air is brought in through ventilation shafts.

Your work space can be cramped, so you should not fear tight and enclosed spaces. It may be necessary to crawl on your hands and knees or work on your back or stomach to do your job. The temperatures can be uncomfortably hot or cold. Some mines are completely dry, while others sometimes have several inches of water on the floor. You may encounter high noise levels and possible hazards such as explosions from gas, falling rocks, fires, machinery and electric accidents, slipping and falling, suffocation, and exposure to poisonous materials. This is one job in which you will always wear a hard hat as well as other safety equipment.

Mine safety has improved greatly in recent years, but mining is still one of the more hazardous industries. State legislation to make mines safer began in the late 1800s, while federal legislation was not initiated until the early 1900s. It is not legislation alone that has made mines much safer workplaces. It is also through the efforts of unions and mining companies.

Special Qualifications for Mining Jobs

Being a miner requires you to be adventurous, flexible, and safety conscious. You already answered questions in Chapter 1 to determine whether you possessed the same characteristics as most hard-hat wearers. Now consider these additional questions to determine if a job in mining is right for you:

1. Are you willing to work in a job where there is an element of danger?
2. Can you handle a work environment that may be noisy, dusty, wet, hot, cold, cramped, or otherwise uncomfortable?
3. Are you willing to work twelve-hour shifts and more than forty hours a week? (The average workweek is forty-four hours.)
4. Are you a quick thinker?
5. Can you work at a fast pace to meet production goals?

In addition to possessing these attributes, underground miners cannot be claustrophobic or panic easily.

Careers Working in Mines

Today's mines use increasingly sophisticated machines and technologies, and few people actually dig ore from the ground. Most miners now operate equipment or work in skilled craft and repair occupations. The majority of these jobs can be entered after completing high school and receiving on-the-job training. Some jobs, however, require advanced technical training or college degrees.

Mining Engineers

If you choose a career as a mining engineer, you will follow in some famous footsteps. President Herbert Hoover began his career in this relatively small profession, which even now numbers fewer than five thousand engineers. Only half of all mining engineers work in the mining industry; the other half work in government agencies, manufacturing industries, or engineering and consulting firms. As a mining engineer within the industry, you will probably work at the location of natural deposits, often near small communities and sometimes outside the United States. If you would enjoy living in Nevada, Colorado, Arizona, West Virginia, or Wyoming, this may be a great profession for you—one-third of all mining engineers live in these states.

The Work of Mining Engineers

Mining engineers find, extract, and prepare coal, metals, and other minerals for use by manufacturing industries and utilities. They design open-pit and underground mines, supervise the construction of mine shafts and tunnels in underground operations, and devise methods for transporting minerals to processing plants. Mining engineers are responsible for the safe, economical, and environmentally sound operation of mines. Some mining engineers work with geologists and metallurgical engineers to locate and appraise new ore deposits. Others develop new mining equipment or direct mineral processing operations to separate minerals from the dirt, rock, and other materials with which they are mixed. Mining engineers frequently specialize in the mining of substances such as coal or gold. With increased emphasis on protecting the environment, many mining engineers work to solve problems related to land reclamation and water and air pollution.

Job Qualifications and Training

Most entry-level positions for mining engineers require at least a bachelor's degree in engineering, which can take from four to six years to achieve. Those who take longer usually participate in cooperative education programs or take electives outside of their major fields. Mining engineers also need to become certified to work in most states. While certification requirements vary, they usually include graduation from an approved engineering program, four years of work experience, and passing a state examination. Canadian engineers need a provincial or territorial license. A master's or a doctoral degree is required if you plan to go into a mining research position. In addition, most mining engineers continue their education by attending workshops, taking courses, and reading professional journals.

Job Outlook and Earnings

Employment of mining engineers is expected to grow about as fast as average after several years of decline. A strong growth in demand for minerals is expected, which will contribute to some employment growth over the next ten years. Additionally, more job openings are likely, as a large number of mining engineers are of retirement age, and many have transferred to other occupations. In addition, there are few graduates of mining engineer programs to fill open positions. Mining operations around the world recruit engineering graduates from the United States, and job opportunities may be more plentiful outside of the country. As a result, graduates should be prepared for the possibility of frequent travel or even living abroad.

Median annual earnings of mining engineers are about $72,000, with the middle 50 percent earning between $54,000 and $94,000. The lowest 10 percent earns about $42,000, and the highest 10 percent earns more than $128,000. In the federal government, mining engineers in supervisory, nonsupervisory, and management positions average about $79,000 a year. According to a recent survey by the National Association of Colleges and Employers, bachelor's degree candidates in mining engineering receive average starting offers of $54,400 a year.

On the Job with a Mining Engineer

Thomas Lien looks upon the mining industry as so vital to the U.S. economy that without it we would be back in prehistoric times. He points out that the mining of metals and other minerals has made possible modern transportation, the production of great quantities of food, the manufacture of our vast range of goods and chemical products, and the development of diverse energy sources to power our machines. Thomas is proud to have been part of the mining industry since the day he graduated from college.

Thomas put himself on the fast path to success as a mining engineer by learning about mineral processing while working in flotation during his college years. He worked part-time during the summers before he graduated with a bachelor's degree in geology with a mining option. This job helped prepare him for several of his future positions, and his degree in geology gave him the flexibility to work in a variety of areas within the mining industry.

First Jobs. It was as cold as Minnesota can be when representatives of the Kennecott Copper Corporation interviewed Thomas for a job in Arizona. The weather may have played a small role in his decision to take the job as a geologist in a warmer climate. His new workplace was an open-pit copper mine, where he examined rocks to discover what minerals they contained. Then he drew detailed geologic maps of their locations so the deposits could be mined more efficiently. Thomas also explored beyond the pit so his company would know about other copper deposits in the area for future expansion. Thomas wore a hard hat in the open pit; however, when he explored new areas, he often wore a wide-brimmed hat to ward off the scorching 110-degree summer heat.

Thomas's boss supervised him closely at first, and they even mapped some areas together. As Thomas gained expertise and his boss became comfortable with his work, he began to do his job independently. This is the way most mining engineers learn their jobs.

After a year as a geologist, Thomas transferred to a concentrator operation that crushed ore until it had the consistency of powder. The addition of water and chemical reagents to the ore made the copper float to the top so it could be recovered. This job tied in nicely with Thomas's earlier part-time work conducting flotation research. It also provided his first supervisory experience with hourly employees.

In this new job, Thomas was fortunate to work under a mill superintendent who believed in helping promising young engineers by giving them responsibility. He assigned Thomas the important task of being responsible for weekend concentrator operation. First, he had to memorize a flow-sheet book that described the function of each piece of machinery in the concentrator operation and how the pieces worked together. Memorizing the book was not enough. He also spent hours studying the machinery so that he could devise a solution whenever a problem occurred. His effort to establish rapport with the plant operators allowed him to gain their valuable input on solutions before he had to run them by a senior manager. Thomas learned how to work well with operation employees and how to earn their respect, skills essential for him to advance in management.

Thomas used his developing managerial skills as he planned and directed the work of two supervisors, twenty-two salaried technicians, and six hourly union employees engaged in production control, production count, sampling, and assaying. About half of the time on the job, Thomas worked in the mine to conduct quality control talks with mine operators.

A Move to Another Mining Company. After two years as a quality control engineer, Thomas determined that falling copper prices and employee layoffs would make it difficult for him to advance at the Kennecott Copper Corporation. He answered a newspaper job advertisement and was soon employed as a process engineer with Kaiser Steel Corporation at the Eagle Mountain Iron Mine. This mine was located in the California desert in a spot that only received two inches of rain a year. Thomas believed that there would be opportunity for advancement with this company, which proved to be true. He remained with Kaiser for seven years.

After working as a process engineer for two years, Thomas became responsible for the operation of a crushing plant at an iron ore beneficiation complex that turned nonmagnetic raw iron ore into a product that could be used in blast furnaces in the steel industry. He worked without direct supervision, using his knowledge of geology, mining, and mineral processing and spending most of his day in the plant.

After less than a year as a superintendent of beneficiation, Thomas made a career leap to a job with much greater technical complexity and a larger workforce. He assumed charge of the pelletizing of iron ore in a plant where he directed eleven supervisors and 220 hourly union employees. Every sixth weekend, he managed the entire mine operation as well as the nearby private mining community. Thomas spent much of his job ensuring the high quality of the pellets to be used in Japanese blast furnaces. Four years later, Thomas believed that Kaiser was running out of iron ore at the site and that he would need to find a new job.

A Move to an Office Job. After twelve years in the field wearing a hard hat and working all day in mines or processing plants, Thomas moved to an office job at Mountain States Mineral Enterprises. This company designed and built ore processing plants for other mining companies. Thomas joined the firm as a senior process engineer, working in research and development.

Curiously, he was working in his new job for the same boss he once had at the copper concentrator nine years before. After just a year, Thomas's managerial talent led to his assignment as operations superintendent with responsibility for all laboratory and pilot plant projects. Then, once again, the mineral industry declined, and Thomas faced taking a wage cut or finding another job.

The Years at Amax Coal. When Thomas made his next move to Amax Coal in Wyoming, he discovered how small the mining industry is. He found himself again working with a former colleague—a Kaiser peer who was his new boss. This job as manager of preparation and quality control at the Belle Ayr Mine was similar to his job at the Kaiser crushing plant. He was responsible for a coal preparation facility that crushed two- to three-foot lumps of coal into two-inch pieces.

At Amax, Thomas has rapidly climbed the career ladder in the following positions:

- Manager, Preparation and Quality Control
- General Mine Manager, Belle Ayr
- Director, Surface Operations Development
- General Manager, Western Operations
- Senior Vice President, Operations
- President, Amax Coal West, later RAG Coal West

Each move up the career ladder involved more time in the office and less time in mines and plant operation. Thomas's hard hat now spends about 85 percent of the time on the hat rack.

Career Advice. Thomas has had a successful career in this field. He advises young mining engineers to learn how to earn the respect of the hourly workers because these employees know the practical side of mining that is not taught in books. Many times early in his career, Thomas's good relationships with hourly workers kept him from making costly mistakes that could have hurt his career.

A Career in Mining: A Female Perspective

It is no longer unusual for women to have careers in mining. In the coal mine where Cindy Wageman is a pit coordinator (supervisor), about 13 percent of the hourly technicians are women. In the Powder River Basin as a whole, 15 to 20 percent of the workers are women. While most are truck drivers, many operate auxiliary pieces of equipment, such as dozers, motor graders, shovels, and drills. In addition, some women work as blasters, mechanics, and plant operators. Each year, more and more women enter the mining industry.

Cindy started wearing a hard hat even before she graduated from college with a bachelor's degree in mining engineering. For one semester, she worked most of the time underground in a coal mine as part of a cooperative education program. Every morning she would don a hard hat with cap lamp, hard-toed boots, safety glasses, and overalls and hook a self-rescuer on her belt. The self-rescuer was to be used in case of fire because it would convert the fire's poisonous carbon monoxide into nonpoisonous carbon dioxide. Dressed for safety, Cindy would walk down a slope to the bottom of the mine, where she would take a small passenger electric car, like a trolley, to the work site with the rest of the crew. The site was a traditional room-and-pillar mining area—pillars (blocks of coal) are left in place to support the roof. The rooms are created when the coal is dug with continuous-mining machines and loaded into shuttle cars.

At this particular mine, the crew consisted of the miner operator, two shuttle operators, two roof bolters installing roof supports, one mechanic, a supervisor or foreman, and a laborer. Cindy's job involved conducting a time study of the various operations, such as how long it took to load a shuttle car and for the car to return to the mining site. She would travel underground every day for about two weeks and then spend time above ground writing reports detailing the time-study observations.

Health and Safety Training Coordinator. Cindy's experience in the cooperative education program proved extraordinarily helpful in landing her first job after graduation conducting time studies in a different underground coal mine. After this job, Cindy left her hard hat behind when she moved into a series of office jobs, including processing permits for a consulting firm and coordinating a statewide program that provided health and safety training for mine workers throughout the state. Her safety job provided her with the opportunity to observe health and safety practices in numerous mines. Along the way, she also earned a master's degree in secondary education.

After working as the training program coordinator for several years, Cindy worked for a large surface coal mine that produced about eighteen million tons of coal per year and moved about thirty-six million yards of overburden (dirt). The overburden is about two hundred feet thick. It is mined in benches (layers) fifty feet thick. Before it is mined, it has to be drilled and blasted. After the layers of overburden are mined, the coal is exposed. Like the overburden, the coal must be drilled and blasted before it can be mined. The coal is actually two seams that total about a hundred feet thick. After the coal is mined, it is hauled to the plant to be stored in silos and then loaded onto coal trains. Both the overburden and coal are mined using large electric shovels and hauled with large trucks. Other mine equipment includes drills, motor graders (blades), rubber tire dozers, track dozers, and water trucks. The mine operates twenty-four hours a day, every day of the year.

Cindy's first position with the surface coal mine was in the training department. She developed courses, taught mandatory health and safety training, and wrote training manuals for various pieces of equipment. After a few years in training, Cindy transferred to engineering, where she handled both short-range and long-range planning. She was also accountable for end-of-month figures and special projects. While in the training and engineering departments, she often spent time in the field.

Relief Coordinator/Production Engineer. Recently, Cindy took a position as relief coordinator/production engineer in the company's production department. Cindy supervises about twenty-two pit technicians, including shovel, dozer, and blade operators; truck drivers; drillers; and blasters. Her days are long, as shifts last twelve hours, and she must complete preliminary work before the day shift begins. At 4:30 A.M., she meets with the night shift coordinator and reviews plans for the upcoming shift with a quick pit tour. A preshift meeting with the maintenance department at 5 A.M. lets her know which machines will be unavailable for the upcoming shift. She sets job assignments, and the actual working shift begins at 6 A.M.

Cindy drives around the site to oversee every aspect of the operation—from where the overburden is dug and dumped to where the coal is mined to when it goes onto the trains. She also attends meetings throughout the shift and coordinates the amount and type of coal being dug with the trains scheduled to pick it up and deliver it to customers. Her pickup truck is her main office, and the mine radio is her telephone. Computers on some of the equipment allow her to monitor production on a real-time basis from the computer in her office. Because the mine uses a team approach, the shovel operators, coal teams, and dirt teams organize much of their own work. Cindy enjoys the fast pace and multiple responsibilities of her job and plans to continue her career in this line of work.

Mining Technicians

Technicians are the right-hand assistants of engineers, geologists, geophysicists, chemists, and metallurgists in the mining industry.

They help in the exploration of mines by collecting and identifying rock samples, surveying sites, and making maps and charts.
They work in laboratories to test rock and ore samples, and they
assist in designing the mines. They also work in mines as shift
bosses to supervise as many as fifty miners, train new miners, and
supervise mine safety operations.

Job Qualifications and Training

Preparation for this position begins in high school with the study
of mathematics, chemistry, and physics. After high school, many
future technicians enroll in a two-year mining technology program that leads to an associate's degree. They take career-specific
courses in mathematics, geology, metallurgy, physics, chemistry,
and technical writing. During the summer, many get a better picture of the mining industry and the area in which they would like
to specialize by participating in internship programs.

Many technicians are offered jobs by companies where they
intern. In addition, recruiters often visit schools that offer mining
technology programs. Technicians also find jobs by applying
directly to the companies where they want to work. However, the
job outlook for technicians is poor due to the decreasing number
of mining operations in the United States.

Technicians usually begin as assistants to professionals working
in exploration, development, and mining operations. As they continue to learn, they advance to jobs with more responsibilities.
They can advance to positions as superintendents and mine managers, and a few become consultants. With additional education,
technicians can become mining engineers.

Mining, Quarrying, and Tunneling Occupations

Many different kinds of workers are needed in the mining industry. Formerly, most jobs could be entered right out of high school

or after workers had gained some experience on the job. Today, more technical training is needed as most jobs are in equipment operation and skilled craft and repair occupations. Here is a brief description of basic jobs in mining that will require you to wear a hard hat:

- **Rock splitters.** Separate blocks of rough dimension stone from quarry mass using jackhammers, wedges, and feathers.
- **Roof bolters.** Operate self-propelled machines to install roof support bolts in underground mines.
- **Mining-machine operators.** Operate mining machinery such as self-propelled or truck-mounted drilling machines, continuous-mining machines, channeling machines, and cutting machines to extract coal, metal and nonmetal ores, rock, stone, or sand from underground or surface sites.
- **Continuous-mining-machine operators.** Operate self-propelled mining machines that rip coal, metal and nonmetal ores, rock, stone, or sand from the face and load it onto conveyors or into shuttle cars in a continuous operation.
- **Mine-cutting- and channeling-machine operators.** Operate machines that cut or channel along the face or seams of coal mines, stone quarries, or other mining surfaces to facilitate blasting, separating, or removing materials.
- **Dragline operators.** Scoop earth away to expose metal or coal.
- **Loading-machine operators.** Rip ore from seams and dump it into trucks.
- **Dredge operators.** Operate dredges to mine sand, gravel, and other materials.
- **Shift bosses.** Oversee all operations at the mine.

Job Outlook and Earnings
Technological advances are increasing productivity in the industry—and are leading to the decline of available jobs. In addition,

many U.S. mining operations will close because other countries can offer lower labor costs and fewer government regulations.

The average salary in mining is higher than that in any other industry. Miners who work underground earn more per hour than those who work on the surface. About 26 percent of all mine workers are union workers (compared with only 15 percent of workers throughout private industry). Of all the nonsupervisory workers in mining and quarrying, coal miners have the highest earnings, averaging more than $1,093 a week. Metal miners follow with an income of more than $975 a week, and other mineral miners earn close to $860 a week. Canadian mine workers earn an average of CAN$900 per week.

For More Information

High school students interested in careers as mining engineers should contact the resources listed for civil engineers at the end of Chapter 2.

More information about careers and training in the mining industry is available from the following organizations:

Mining Association of Canada
350 Sparks Street, Suite 1105
Ottawa, ON K1R 7S8
Canada
www.mining.ca

National Mining Association
101 Constitution Avenue NW, Suite 500 East
Washington, DC 20001
www.nma.org

Society for Mining, Metallurgy, and Exploration
8307 Shaffer Parkway
Littleton, CO 80127
www.smenet.org

United Mine Workers of America
8315 Lee Highway
Fairfax, VA 22031
www.umwa.org

CHAPTER FIVE

Careers in Manufacturing

ave you ever wondered how a car is built? What about an airplane? Or maybe you are curious to know how the bowl of cereal you had this morning was processed and packaged. A career in manufacturing will provide you the capability of learning just how that nut and bolt or grain of flour becomes an everyday item that we rely so heavily upon. As you can imagine, not all jobs associated with the process and manufacturing of the items require a hard hat; however, as individual employee safety becomes a major corporate concern, you might be surprised how many jobs do require this type of protection.

The History of U.S. Manufacturing

You might remember from your world history class that the Industrial Revolution brought modern manufacturing to the forefront. However, it was not until World War I, when industries expanded to make war materials, that the United States became the number one producer of manufactured goods.

By the middle of the twentieth century, one in every three Americans worked in manufacturing, and only 12 percent of Americans still earned a living on the farm. In the 1970s, the global economy had a devastating impact on American manufacturing industries, when prices for their products increased and demand for them declined. This caused many American manufacturing companies to lay off workers, and some even had to shut down or move overseas. The manufacturing workforce was further reduced by automation, which introduced computer-controlled equipment to help manufacturing reach higher levels of efficiency. Today, efficiency continues to be increased within manufacturing by the implementation of lean manufacturing. This methodology reviews the current process and determines how to reduce waste through less human effort, less manufacturing space, less investment in tools, and less engineering time to develop products.

Where the Jobs Are

Factory jobs traditionally have been located close to steel mills in northern states, but manufacturing plants can now be found throughout the country. A career in manufacturing can mean working in gigantic firms such as Caterpillar, U.S. Steel, or Ford Motor Company, but it also means working for medium-size or even quite small companies. Some of the major manufacturing industries include aerospace, motor vehicle and equipment, steel, and food production. These industries offer just a portion of the many hard-hat job opportunities found in a country that makes everything from locomotives to tin cans.

The variety of manufacturing jobs is mind-boggling. You will probably start as an entry-level worker, climb the career ladder to team leader, advance to foreman or supervisor, and then possibly reach the level of plant supervisor or even manager. Most skills are taught through on-the-job training, except for special skills that require additional training, such as welding.

Careers in the Aerospace Industry

If you are fascinated by outer space, you may want to consider an exciting career in one of the two segments that make up the aerospace industry. The largest segment produces aircraft, engines, and related parts, while the smaller segment produces guided missiles, space vehicles, propulsion units, and parts. Approximately eighteen hundred establishments make up the aerospace industry in the United States, from the very large Boeing Corporation, which manufactures airplanes, to a small company making parts for space vehicles.

The Sky Is the Limit with Aerospace Jobs

A job building a jet or a space shuttle or parts for one of these machines usually requires wearing a hard hat on the factory floor. In this industry, entry-level workers rub elbows with coworkers who are skilled enough to work on the leading edge of technology. While there are far more small firms than large ones in the aerospace industry, most employees work for companies that employ more than a thousand workers. Also, you are most likely to have a production-related job within the industry: more than 40 percent are employed in production; installation, maintenance, and repair; and transportation and material-moving occupations. Table 1 shows the wide variety of jobs in aerospace.

TABLE I. Employment of wage and salary workers in aerospace product and parts manufacturing by occupation, 2006, and projected change, 2006–2016			
OCCUPATION *(Employment in thousands)*	EMPLOYMENT, 2006 NUMBER	PERCENT	PERCENT CHANGE
All occupations	472	100	5.4
Management, business, and financial occupations	81	17.2	4.9
General and operations managers	4	0.9	-8.3
Financial managers	2	0.5	1.8
Industrial production managers	5	1	1.8
Engineering managers	10	2.2	12

Purchasing agents, except wholesale, retail, farm products	10	2	1.8
Cost estimators	2	0.5	10
Human resources, training, labor-relations specialists	3	0.7	10
Logisticians	4	0.8	12
Management analysts	9	1.8	1.8
Business operation specialists, all other	9	1.9	12
Accountants and auditors	4	0.9	1.8
Budget analysts	3	0.6	1.8
Professional and related occupations	**147**	**31.2**	**8.9**
Computer software engineers, applications	12	2.4	22.2
Computer software engineers, systems software	5	1.2	12
Computer systems analysts	3	0.6	12
Aerospace engineers	44	9.3	6.9
Electrical and electronics engineers	5	1	1.8
Industrial engineers, including health and safety	15	3.2	22.8
Industrial engineers	15	3.1	23.7
Mechanical engineers	11	2.3	1.8
Engineers, all other	9	1.8	1.8
Drafters	5	1.1	8.9
Aerospace engineering and operations technicians	4	0.8	1.8
Electrical and electronic engineering technicians	3	0.6	1.8
Industrial engineering technicians	7	1.5	12
Engineering technicians, except drafters, all other	5	1.1	1.8
Office and administrative support occupations	**38**	**8**	**-3.2**
Bookkeeping, accounting, and auditing clerks	2	0.5	1.8

Production, planning, and expediting clerks	7	1.6	1.8
Shipping, receiving, and traffic clerks	4	0.8	-2
Stock clerks and order fillers	5	1	-14.8
Secretaries and administrative assistants	8	1.8	-0.6
Office clerks, general	4	0.8	0.3
Installation, maintenance, and repair occupations	**41**	**8.7**	**14.3**
Avionics technicians	4	0.9	12
Electrical and electronics repairers	2	0.5	8.6
Aircraft mechanics and service technicians	21	4.4	22.2
Industrial machinery mechanics	2	0.5	17.1
Maintenance and repair workers	4	0.8	1.8
Production occupations	**141**	**29.9**	**2.5**
First-line supervisors/managers	9	2	1.8
Aircraft structure, surfaces, rigging, and systems assemblers	24	5.2	12
Electrical and electronic equipment assemblers	4	0.8	-18.5
Team assemblers	7	1.5	1.8
Computer-controlled machine tool operators	5	1.2	12
Machine tool cutting setters, operators, and tenders	12	2.6	-6.5
Machinists	18	3.8	6.9
Multiple machine tool setters, operators, and tenders	4	0.8	12
Tool and die makers	3	0.7	6.9
Welders, cutters, solderers, brazers	4	0.8	8.3
Inspectors, testers, sorters, samplers, weighers	16	3.5	-4

Note: Columns may not add to totals due to omission of occupations with small employment

Source: U.S. Department of Labor, Bureau of Labor Statistics, 2007

Here is some more detailed information about a few of the careers listed in the table.

- **Aerospace engineers** design, develop, and test aircraft, spacecraft, and missiles and supervise the manufacturing of these products.
- **Aircraft assemblers** usually specialize in one assembly task and work with hundreds of other assemblers to install parts of airplanes, space vehicles, or missiles, such as wings or landing gear.
- **Machinists** follow blueprints to make parts to specification when they can't be mass-produced due to the small number needed. They are highly skilled workers.
- **Tool and die makers** study blueprints to determine specifications for the pieces they are shaping. Then they cut or punch out the needed pieces and attach them with bolts, rivets, or other devices.
- **Inspectors, testers, sorters, samplers, and weighers** perform safety checks and are responsible for quality control.

Many of the other jobs in the aerospace industry are in administrative support, clerical, and service occupations.

Job Qualifications and Training

If you select a hard-hat career in the aerospace industry, you should plan on keeping up with the constant technological advances and changes being made in the field. This is true whether you are an entry-level worker with a high school diploma or an aerospace engineer with an advanced college degree. While most production jobs can be entered without education beyond high school, you need mechanical aptitude and good eye-hand coordination. Unskilled production workers receive on-the-job instruction from their coworkers as well as formal training sessions and classes. However, apprenticeships are required to become fully qualified for many highly skilled jobs. Some apprenticeships can take up to four years to complete.

Job Outlook and Earnings

Overall employment within aerospace is expected to grow 7 percent over the next ten years. This is about as fast as the growth rate for all other occupations. While job prospects will vary by specialty and location, depending on the health and composition of local industry, opportunities will be best for individuals with an associate's degree or extensive job training in engineering technology. As technology changes and becomes more sophisticated, employers will continue to look for technicians who are skilled in new technology and require little additional training. An increase in the number of jobs related to public health and safety should create job opportunities for engineering technicians with the appropriate training and certification. In addition, many job openings will stem from the need to replace technicians who retire or leave the labor force. Nevertheless, projected growth is tied to federal defense expenditures, commercial aircraft sales, and exports.

Jobs in aerospace manufacturing pay better than their counterparts in many other areas of manufacturing. Aerospace engineers have median annual salaries of about $67,000. Weekly earnings for production workers averaged $1,153 in aerospace product parts manufacturing in 2006, compared with $691 in all manufacturing and $568 in all private industry. In Canada, the weekly average rate is around CAN$1,000. The higher pay is due to the higher levels of skill and responsibility required in aerospace jobs. In addition, union membership is higher in aerospace jobs: slightly more than 20 percent of all workers in the aircraft and parts sector, along with 12 percent of workers in the guided missiles and space vehicles sectors, are union members or covered by union contracts, compared to 13 percent of all workers throughout private industry. Canada's union membership is 49 percent for aerospace jobs, compared to 32 percent for all occupations.

Careers in Motor Vehicle and Equipment Manufacturing

Motor vehicles play a central role in the lives of most Americans. Buses transport children to school and workers to their jobs. Cars take people everywhere from shopping malls to vacation spots. Businesses depend on motor vehicles to transport products across the country. In fact, the United States is the world's largest marketplace for motor vehicles. There are more than 243 million motor vehicles—136 million passenger cars and 107 million trucks—in the United States. To satisfy this demand, large assembly plants employ thousands of workers, and smaller plants manufacture parts and accessories. In addition, the motor vehicle and equipment industry contributes to employment in such areas as motor vehicle dealerships, automotive repair shops, gasoline service stations, highway construction companies, and public transit companies. Table 2 shows the distribution of motor vehicle and equipment manufacturing by activity.

TABLE 2. Percent distribution of employment and establishments in motor vehicle and parts manufacturing by detailed industry sector, 2006

INDUSTRY SECTOR	EMPLOYMENT	ESTABLISHMENTS
Motor vehicle parts manufacturing	60.9	68.6
Motor vehicle manufacturing	22.6	5.1
Motor vehicle body and trailer manufacturing	16.5	26.3

Source: U.S. Department of Labor, Bureau of Labor Statistics, 2007

Work Hazards and Conditions

If you decide to work in the motor vehicle and equipment manufacturing industry, be prepared for long hours and shifts. You may also encounter uncomfortable working conditions that include heat, fumes, noise, and a greater potential for injury and illness than that in most other industries.

Half of all jobs in the motor vehicle and equipment industry are located in Michigan, Ohio, and Indiana, but California, New York, Illinois, Missouri, North Carolina, Tennessee, and Wisconsin are home to a significant number of jobs. More than 51 percent of motor vehicle and equipment manufacturing jobs are in firms with more than a thousand workers.

Manufacturing Cars and Equipment: More than Just an Assembly Line

You are probably aware of the assembly-line opportunities in this industry. Assembly-line workers are the most common workers in the automotive manufacturing industry. Henry Ford pioneered the use of assembly-line methods in making the famous Model T cars.

Today's assembly lines are much more sophisticated, with robots working side by side with people putting together the parts of manufactured products. Products usually move from station to station, where one or more tasks are performed, such as adding, tightening, welding, or inspecting a part. The product continues in assembly-line fashion until the car, truck, or bus is complete. This same manufacturing method is used for making other products—from refrigerators to toys.

However, the manufacture of motor vehicles involves many other kinds of jobs. The process begins with designers who sketch an image of the vehicle in close cooperation with individuals in marketing, production, and engineering. Here's a snapshot of some of the many workers involved in bringing us all kinds of motor vehicles.

- **Engineers** are involved with a variety of specialties. Mechanical engineers research, develop, design, and oversee the production of motor vehicle engines, transmissions, brakes, and other mechanical equipment. Electrical and electronics engineers design, develop, test, and supervise the manufacture of motor vehicle electrical systems. Industrial engineers concentrate on the best way to use workers, machinery, and materials to create motor vehicles and equipment.

- **Engineering technicians** support engineers in all aspects of their jobs. Most specialize in a certain area, such as design, development, research, or testing.
- **Supervisors** oversee skilled craft workers, assembly-line workers, and laborers. While in the past they exercised their authority to direct the efforts of the workers, increasingly plants have adopted the team approach in getting work done. Supervisors now act more as facilitators for groups or teams of workers, aiding in group decision making and conflict resolution.
- **Floor assemblers** use soldering irons or power drills to install or fasten parts onto the vehicles as they pass by on the assembly line.
- **Bench assemblers** are usually responsible for a specific part at their work areas, especially in equipment factories. The product does not pass quickly in front of them; instead, it remains until the entire product is complete. Bench assemblers may also test the product they have assembled.
- **Precision assemblers** are highly skilled workers who assemble a wide range of finished products from manufactured parts or subassemblies. They produce intricate manufactured products for motor vehicles and other equipment as well as for aircraft, computers, and small electrical and electronic components. They may complete the final assembly or work on difficult subassemblies.
- **Machine assemblers** perform assembly work at a lower skill level than that required of precision assemblers. Machine

assemblers work on such things as air-conditioning coils, ball bearing rings, fuel injection units, and subassemblies.

- **Machine setters, operators, and tenders** run the machines that make the bodies and parts of motor vehicles.
- **Welders and welding-machine operators** may perform manual welding, in which the work is entirely controlled by the welder, or semiautomatic welding, in which the welder uses machinery to help perform welding tasks.

Job Outlook and Earnings

Employment is expected to decline in the manufacture of motor vehicles and equipment. Worldwide competition has increased factory automation and worker productivity, resulting in the need for fewer employees. Only engineers needed to design more innovative products and procedures can expect job growth in this industry. While overall employment will decrease, a substantial need will remain for workers to replace those who are retiring or moving to other jobs.

As in the aerospace industry, wages are relatively high for those involved in the manufacture of motor vehicles and equipment. At $1,213 per week, earnings of production workers in establishments that manufacture complete motor vehicles were among the highest in the nation in 2006. Workers in establishments that make motor vehicle parts averaged $904 weekly, and those in motor vehicle body and trailer manufacturing averaged $683 per week, compared with $691 for workers in all manufacturing industries and $568 for those in the entire private sector. Canadian employees in this field have similar weekly wage rates.

On the Job with an Automobile Assembly Plant Worker

It isn't easy to get a job on the assembly line at a New United Motor Manufacturing, Inc., (NUMMI) plant that makes cars in a joint venture between General Motors and Toyota. After turning in her application, Gayle Bowen had to take mechanical and math tests, be interviewed informally, and take blood and urine tests—all on the same day. Then, one week later, interviewers called her back for another series of tests. She fastened nuts and bolts together as fast as she could on a simulation test and adhered tape to the side of a car to show she could align the tape so the car could be painted. Another test confirmed her ability to follow instructions exactly. The next week, Gayle returned and joined five other job applicants in trying to solve problems together to show they could work as a team. Finally, after a personal interview and a physical examination, she landed a job on the assembly line.

Hard hats are not required for all jobs in auto assembly plants, but they are absolutely essential for those who work on chassis assembly lines, as Gayle does. Much of this work takes Gayle under the vehicles, and she constantly faces the possibility of hitting her head on hanging parts or having something fall on her head. Gayle bumps her hard hat on car parts all day long. In addition to a hard hat, she also wears safety glasses and steel-toed shoes.

Gayle began her career at NUMMI on the assembly line as part of a five-person team that set windshields into cars. The line only stopped when it was time for a break or a meal or when there were problems with the machinery. Gayle worked for two and one-half hours between each line stop for fifteen-minute breaks or forty-five-minute mealtimes.

Her first job was to attach a vehicle's left-side molding in only fifty-eight seconds. Before she ever stepped foot on the floor, she learned about company policies, labor relations, standardized work, and teamwork during a week of orientation. When she was ready to work, Gayle spent the first hour watching how workers attached a left-side molding onto the cars. She read through a manifest—a large sheet of paper with instructions for building the vehicle—so she would know a Corolla from a Prizm and could identify their specific parts. Gradually, throughout the day, she learned how to do her job under the supervision of the team leader. For three days, the team leader stayed with her, offering help as needed. Within sixty days, Gayle had learned all five of the team jobs.

Climbing the Plant Career Ladder. After one and a half years as a windshield assembler, Gayle went to the final line and worked on car interiors. During this time, she also took her first step up the plant career ladder by becoming a team leader. To acquire this position, she went through a selection process and attended class for forty hours on her own time to learn leadership techniques.

Her next career move was to a position as a quality assurance team member. In this job, she worked by herself to check more than a hundred items on finished cars. When she found a defect, she usually repaired it herself. To advance her career, Gayle became a Toyota production systems trainer, working with both new hires and team leaders. Then she became a member of the pilot team, a challenging job that lasts only through a model change. Pilot team members make sure that new models can be built smoothly on the different lines. As part of this job, Gayle traveled to Japan to observe workers there, and then she returned and revamped processes in her plant.

When her job on the pilot team ended, Gayle returned to the production floor with a promotion to group leader. To earn this position, she asked her manager for a recommendation to the company's associate program. Before she could function as a group leader, supervising four team leaders and twenty assemblers, she took a fourteen-week in-house class that covered all areas of manufacturing. It particularly stressed practical problem solving, safety issues, and human relations.

Gayle is interested in further advancing her career. The next step will be for her to become an assistant manager—a position that involves supervising five group leaders. After this step, she could advance to manager and supervise the five assistant managers in the chassis area. As the following organization list shows, promotion to general manager and then plant manager are the next steps in the career hierarchy at NUMMI.

- Assembler (entry level)
- Team Leader
- Group Leader
- Assistant Manager
- Manager
- General Manager
- Plant Manager

Safety First. One of the most important aspects of Gayle's job as group leader is to ensure the safety of every worker in her area. Before the assembly line starts, she often speaks to team leaders about safety issues. She also looks for ways to make each job safer. At times, she steps in and shows an assembler a safer way to complete a job, and she enforces safety regulations by penalizing people who fail to wear the proper safety gear. Although Gayle now has a management job, she must occasionally help out when a team leader is absent or a worker needs to leave the plant floor.

Careers in the Steel Industry

The steel industry has always been important to the growth of our nation and its economy. It produced the steel for the railroad tracks that connected the East to the western frontier and helped in its development. The industry also produced steel for building ships, tanks, and arms used to protect the country during major conflicts in the twentieth century. Steel is a component in constructing skyscrapers and cars, reinforcing roads, and making thousands of other products we use each day—from nails to pots and pans.

After World War II, the importation of cheaper steel from other countries severely affected the steel industry in the United States.

However, recent rapid changes in the U.S. steel industry have helped the industry rebound to lead the world in worker productivity. The industry still faces stiff competition from other countries; however, the steel industry is now in a better position to handle these challenges.

In the past, steel was manufactured in integrated mills that used coal, iron ore, and limestone to produce iron in blast furnaces that was then refined into steel. The development of the electric arc furnace (EAF) has brought fundamental changes to the industry. These furnaces convert scrap metal to steel and have fewer steps in the production process. They are also cheaper to build and operate and do not have to be located close to raw materials. Almost half of all steel now comes from EAFs.

Increasing competition from abroad and in the domestic market has spurred integrated and EAF steel producers to modernize and use more sophisticated equipment. As a result, workers are often required to learn new skills. These changes have emphasized flexibility and adaptability for both workers and equipment. Competition from abroad has also resulted in the increasing specialization of steel production so producers can find different specialty markets for their goods.

Work Hazards and Conditions

When you think of working in a steel mill, you probably think of a job that is strenuous, hot, noisy, and potentially dangerous. While many jobs are still like this, new facilities and equipment have revolutionized the workplace for many. For example, many of the most strenuous tasks are now automated—some equipment can even be operated from remote, air-conditioned rooms. Still, working in the industry carries risks. Cases of occupational injury and illness in the industry were 12 percent of full-time workers a few years ago, significantly higher than the 2006 rates, which were 5.4 percent in iron and steel mills and 8.8 percent in steel product manufacturing. The entire private sector injury rate in 2006 was 4.4 percent. The rate for all of manufacturing was 6 percent.

If you decide to work in steel production, expect to wear a hard hat, glasses, earplugs, steel-toed shoes, and other protective clothing in most areas.

Half of all steel mills employ more than a thousand workers. In addition, the industry is still concentrated in Pennsylvania, Ohio, and Indiana, although the introduction of EAFs has made it possible to find jobs throughout the country.

Due to the expense of plant and machinery and significant production startup costs, most mills operate around the clock, seven days a week. Workers averaged 44.6 hours per week in 2006 in iron and steel mills and 43.7 hours in steel product manufacturing. Workers usually work varying shifts, switching between working days one week and nights the next. Some mills operate two twelve-hour shifts, while others operate three eight-hour shifts. Overtime work during peak production periods is common.

Jobs Qualifications and Training

Steel mills need engineers and scientists to build and design mills and equipment, test and improve the quality of the steel, and develop new specialized metals. Administrative support jobs are also available. However, nearly 80 percent of workers are employed in operator, fabricator, precision production, laborer, craft, and repair jobs. Altogether, more than 154,000 workers are employed in the steel industry.

You can land a job in steel production with a high school diploma, but some of the more skilled positions require community or technical college training. Workers usually learn their jobs by assisting experienced workers and often specialize in a particular process in the production of steel. It typically takes from four to five years to have sufficient experience to obtain a skilled position.

Depending on the company and position in Canada, completion of secondary school is highly recommended. Trade certification is also compulsory in Quebec, Ontario, Saskatchewan,

Alberta, and British Columbia. Interprovincial trade certification (Red Seal) is also available to qualified sheet metal workers.

Job Outlook and Earnings

The number of jobs in the steel industry is expected to continue to decline because of the introduction of labor-saving technologies and equipment. Job opportunities will come from replacing workers who retire or leave the industry. The best job opportunities will be for those able to handle the new, more technologically advanced equipment.

Earnings in the steel industry vary by type of production and occupation but are higher than average earnings in private industry as a whole. Average weekly earnings of nonsupervisory production workers in 2006 were $1,091 in iron and steel mills and $775 in establishments making steel products from purchased steel, compared with $691 in all manufacturing and $568 throughout private industry. As in the United States, employees in Canada will see slightly increased earnings in the steel business over all other occupations. Current weekly averages are around CAN$935.

Earnings in selected occupations in steel manufacturing appear in Table 3.

Table 3. Median hourly earnings of the largest occupations in steel manufacturing, May 2006

OCCUPATION	IRON AND STEEL MILLS	STEEL PRODUCT MANUFACTURING	ALL INDUSTRIES
First-line supervisors/ managers of production and operating workers	$26.75	$23.58	$22.74
Maintenance and repair workers, general	$19.11	$18.16	$15.34
Rolling machine setters, operators, and tenders	$18.41	$15.38	$14.93

Metal-refining furnace operators and tenders	$17.97	$16.36	$15.69
Inspectors, testers, sorters, samplers, and weighers	$17.38	$15.02	$14.14
Crane and tower operators	$17.18	$16.36	$18.77
Laborers and freight, stock, and material movers	$15.51	$10.32	$10.20
Extruding and drawing machine setters, operators, and tenders	$15.28	$15.04	$13.58
Cutting, punching, and press machine setters, operators, and tenders	$15.00	$13.84	$12.66
Helpers—production workers	$12.22	$12.15	$9.97

Source: U.S. Department of Labor, Bureau of Labor Statistics, 2007

On the Job with a Steel Industry Worker

Charles Hubbard has spent the past thirty years in a Gary, Indiana, steel mill, where he held five different jobs. With a high school diploma, he began his career as a member of the labor crew. The company verified his diploma, then gave Charles a test to determine his ability to learn new technical information. Then, he was given thirty days of training before he began his first job sweeping and keeping the mill clean. He wore a hard hat to protect him from falling debris. Charles's next job was as a sheer operator, which involved cutting plates of steel as thick as 110 inches for use in building tanks and battleships.

Charles's third job was working at an open-hearth furnace, a hot and dangerous area where molten metal splashes and spills as steel is being refined. All of the raw materials used to make steel are placed into the huge oxygen furnace. After about twelve minutes at temperatures topping ten thousand degrees, the materials melt to produce a molten metal that is strained and checked for impurities. Once the metal is placed in water, cooled, and allowed to harden to its final density, it becomes steel. Each batch of molten metal produces up to 230 tons of steel.

Charles next worked in the mold foundry, another dangerous area where molten metal is poured into molds to form objects, such as manhole covers, from the hardest steel possible. Items are made with a special cast-iron mold called a hot-top mold. Most molds are open, like a bowl, but a hot-top mold has a lid with a small hole in the center to allow molten metal to be poured in. The circular weight plates used in gyms and weight rooms are also made in mold foundries using hot-top molds. Each plate is carefully poured to be the exact weight specified on the plate.

Today, Charles works in transportation at the steel mill. This is the safest of all his steel jobs, but he still is required to wear a hard hat. He drives a big sweeper truck similar to those used to clean city streets. The trucks are equipped with huge vacuums on each side that suck in as much dust and dirt as possible to keep the mill clean. This reduces the likelihood of impurities infecting the molten metal. The heat of the molten metal will burn off small amounts, but excess amounts can taint the metal.

Workday Challenges. Charles says that one of the toughest aspects of working in a steel mill is braving the intense temperatures every day. In summer, the heat inside the mill can be blistering, reaching temperatures of approximately 170 to 210 degrees in some areas. In winter, the temperature outside is usually the temperature inside because doors are constantly opened to move materials in or out.

To deal with the abnormal temperatures and other safety hazards in a steel mill, Charles and his fellow workers follow mandatory safety precautions. Along with a hard hat, each worker in the mill must wear safety glasses with side shields, hot-metal gloves and suits over thermal underwear or sweats, and safety shoes. These items help protect the entire body from extreme temperature and other hazards.

Although working in a steel mill can be dangerous, Charles feels the wages are good compensation for the risk involved. Furthermore, the union he belongs to works to ensure job safety and security.

Careers in the Food-Processing Industry

The food-processing industry is the bridge that connects farmers and consumers. Workers in this industry turn raw fruit and vegetables, grains, meats, and dairy products into the foods we buy in grocery stores or eat in restaurants. Most of the industry's employees work in plants that produce meat products. Many employees also work in plants that make bakery goods and preserve fruits and vegetables.

Work Hazards and Conditions

Food-processing plants are often noisy and may be cold and damp or very warm. These plants exist in every state, but most of them are located close to where the foods are grown or produced. Workers in food processing often suffer hand, wrist, and elbow injuries due to the repetitive nature of their jobs. Many jobs require standing for long periods and lifting heavy objects. And many workers use potentially dangerous tools and machines to cut, slice, and grind food products.

Some workers in this industry must wear protective clothing, including hard hats, gloves, aprons, and shoes. Safety training and frequent breaks help reduce injuries tied to the dangers that exist in these jobs. Workers in the food-processing industry must be flexible because shift work is common.

Job Outlook and Earnings

In food processing, about 75 percent of employees are production workers—from skilled precision workers to less-skilled machine operators and laborers. Increasing automation is creating a need for more and more machine operators. Most workers are able to learn their jobs in a few days from more experienced workers, and you may not even need a high school diploma to land a job in this industry. Those workers who show they can handle responsibility often become machine operators or are promoted to supervisory positions. Overall, job opportunities should be available in all food-processing specialties due to the need to replace experienced workers who transfer to other occupations or leave the labor force. Rate of growth is expected to increase about as fast as the average for all employment.

The number of hours you work plays a major role in determining your earnings. Production workers average close to $13 per hour, with increased salaries for shift work. Canada's hourly rate for food processors is approximately CAN$14 per hour.

On the Job with a Purchasing Administrator

Russ Day's job in administration requires him to spend most of his time in an office overseeing the purchasing of equipment and materials used in a food-processing plant, but he still wears a hard hat about 20 percent of the time. Whenever he steps inside the plant, he is required by law and by company policy to wear one. The law requires hair to be covered in a food-processing plant, but company policy requires a hard hat.

At Russ's company, the hard hat has another function beyond safety. It is color coded so workers can be easily identified. All of the management employees wear white hard hats, while production workers wear different colors to indicate the areas in which they work.

Russ's job is to observe and check equipment as it operates as well as the quality of food to be processed. He buys fresh produce, such as corn and green beans, flour and shortening for baking, livestock and meat cuts for the meat-processing facility, and milk products for dairy operations. Each of these areas has specialized equipment that has to be purchased and maintained, requiring Russ to gain hands-on knowledge of plant operations.

Careers in Smaller Manufacturing Companies

Within the United States, more than three hundred thousand companies manufacture an enormous array of goods. While most manufacturing jobs are in the large industries described earlier in this chapter, many jobs exist in firms with just a handful of employees. Most of these are light manufacturers that make products such as parts for automobiles and planes. They may also support packaging and refurbishing of products. You could even start your own manufacturing company and become both a hard-hat wearer and an owner.

For More Information

Information about jobs with a particular company can be obtained either by writing to the human resources manager of the company or researching the company's Internet website. Most companies post job openings along with detailed job descriptions and skill requirements right on the company website.

General information about training and work opportunities is available by contacting the following unions:

International Association of Machinists and Aerospace
   Workers (IAM)
9000 Machinists Place
Upper Marlboro, MD 20772
www.goiam.org

United Automobile, Aerospace, and Agricultural Implement
  Workers of America (UAW)
Solidarity House
8000 East Jefferson Avenue
Detroit, MI 48214
www.uaw.org

United Steelworkers
5 Gateway Center
Pittsburgh, PA 15222
www.uswa.org

Career information is also available through trade associations.
For more information, contact:

Aerospace Industries Association
1000 Wilson Boulevard, Suite 1700
Arlington, VA 22209
www.aia-aerospace.org

American Association of Meat Processors
PO Box 269
Elizabethtown, PA 17022
www.aamp.com

American Foundry Society
1695 North Penny Lane
Schaumburg, IL 60173
www.afsinc.org

American Institute of Aeronautics and Astronautics
1801 Alexander Bell Drive, Suite 500
Reston, VA 20191
www.aiaa.org

American Iron and Steel Institute
1140 Connecticut Avenue NW, Suite 705
Washington, DC 20036
www.steel.org

American Meat Institute
1150 Connecticut Avenue NW, Twelfth floor
Washington, DC 20036
www.meatami.org

American Welding Society
550 Northwest LeJeune Road
Miami, Fl 33126
www.amweld.org

Association of International Automobile Manufacturers
2111 Wilson Boulevard, Suite 1150
Arlington, VA 22201
www.aiam.org

Grocery Manufacturers Association
1350 I Street NW, Suite 300
Washington, DC 20005
www.gmaonline.org

National Association of Manufacturers
1331 Pennsylvania Avenue NW
Washington, DC 20004
www.nam.org

National Management Association
2210 Arbor Boulevard
Dayton, OH 45439
www.nma1.org

Satellite Industry Association
1730 M Street NW, Suite 600
Washington, DC 20036
www.sia.org

Tooling & Manufacturing Association
1177 South Dee Road
Park Ridge, IL 60068
www.tmanet.com

Below are some good contacts for more information in Canada:

Canadian Restaurant and Foodservices Association
316 Bloor Street West
Toronto, ON M5S 1W5
Canada
www.crfa.ca

Canadian Steel Trade and Employment Congress
234 Eglinton Avenue East, Suite 501
Toronto, ON M4P 1K7
Canada
www.cstec.ca

Canadian Tooling & Machining Association
140 McGovern Drive, Unit 3
Cambridge, ON N3H 4R7
Canada
www.ctma.com

International Association of Machinists & Aerospace Workers
15 Gervais Drive, Suite 707
North York, ON M3C 1Y8
Canada
www.iamaw.ca

Sheet Metal Workers International Association
1750 New York Avenue NW
Washington, DC 20006
www.smwia.org

CHAPTER SIX

Jobs in the Lumber Industry

The United States has nearly 750,000 acres of forests that can potentially be used for timber. The U.S. produces fifty billion board feet of lumber each year, while Canada produces twenty-two billion board feet. Our forests are a rich natural resource for business. At the same time, our nation's forests provide habitat for wildlife as well as beauty, tranquility, and recreational opportunities for millions of visitors.

The timber harvested from the forests yields wood for an ever-increasing number of products each year. We live in wood houses, sit at wood desks, dine on wood tables, read newspapers and books made from wood pulp, play with wooden toys, write with wood-cased pencils, and burn wood in our fireplaces. The list becomes even longer if you include all the wood products processed with chemicals or in other ways, such as dyes, paints, medicines, soaps, and glues. The lumber industry employs thousands of people to turn trees into lumber and other wood products. A great number of these jobs are held by people wearing hard hats in forests and sawmills.

History of the Lumber Industry

Logging has been an important and exciting industry in the United States since the early days when the forests echoed with the warning cry of "Timber." As settlers moved west, so did the lumber industry. Giant timber companies cut everything in their path and were not concerned about replanting forests because there seemed to be an inexhaustible supply. Since the start of the twentieth century, the lumber industry has changed from one that harvested timber with little regard for future growth to an industry that counts forest management and restoration as key parts of its job. The government and conservation groups have also greatly influenced how and where logging is done. The first public forests were set aside under President Theodore Roosevelt, and more lands have continued to be protected so that today almost one-third of all forest land in the United States is under public ownership.

During the 1960s, a strong concern for the environment and the preservation of forests—especially old-growth trees— emerged in the United States. Since then, the environmental movement has grown stronger, with many groups dedicated to protecting animal habitat as well as unique ecosystems. As a result, many laws closely regulate harvesting trees and reforestation efforts on public and private land. No matter what job hard hatters perform in the forest, they need to follow practices that do minimal damage to the environment.

Today, the U.S. lumber industry is primarily located in the West, South, Northeast, and Great Lakes regions of the country. Canada also produces an impressive supply of lumber. The timber industry hires many different kinds of workers performing a variety of jobs. Nearly sixty-nine thousand tree-cutting and related logging workers in the United States, and about fourteen thousand workers in Canada harvest thousands of acres of forest each year. Approximately twenty thousand forest and conservation workers help develop, maintain, and protect these forests.

Careers in the Logging Industry

The job of being a logger has changed greatly since the early days when trees were cut down by lumberjacks swinging axes and hauled away by teams of oxen. The exploits of loggers in the last half of the nineteenth century were exaggerated in tales of Paul Bunyan and his giant blue ox, Babe. It was said, for example, that Paul had to scoop out the Great Lakes in order to find enough drinking water for Babe.

Today's loggers are assisted by a wide array of mechanical equipment, which has reduced the number of loggers on crews. A variety of workers make up a logging crew. The exact composition of the crew depends on the size of the logs, the terrain, and the technology employed. Crews are generally small—three to six workers—and the more mechanized the operation, the smaller the crew.

In general, logging is far more mechanized in the West than in other regions of the country. Loggers typically do not work for large logging companies but for small subcontractors who have contracted to cut a certain section of trees. The owner frequently works alongside the crew while directing the work.

Here are some of the jobs you will find in a logging operation:

- **General laborers** clear areas of brush and other growth to prepare for logging activities.
- **Fallers** cut down trees with handheld chain saws or mechanical felling equipment.
- **Feller or buncher operators** use a feller/buncher machine to fell trees and lay them on the ground in a specific location.
- **Harvester processors** involved in cut-to-length logging sit inside a cab and maneuver a machine to cut down small trees, pull them through the machine to trim off limbs, and cut the tree into logs. This machine performs the work of several loggers and even has a computer. The operator pushes buttons to direct most of the operation.
- **Buckers** trim off the tops and branches of trees at the felling site or before they are transported at the landing. Fallers may also do this job.

- **Choke setters** fasten chokers (steel cables or chains) around logs to be skidded (dragged) by tractors or forwarded (carried) by cable to the log landing or deck. There logs are separated by species and loaded onto trucks or trains for transport to sawmills or other wood-processing plants. Skidder operators may also do this job.
- **Skidder operators** drive crawlers or wheeled tractors called skidders to drag or transport logs from the felling site in the forest to the log-landing area.
- **Forwarder operators** in cut-to-length logging use a machine to load logs, carry them to the landing area, and put them on trucks.
- **Yarders** run winches to pull logs to the landing area.
- **Heavy-equipment operators** run a variety of equipment. They operate shears to cut logs into desired lengths and grapple loaders to lift and load logs onto trucks and trains. They also operate bulldozers, graders, power shovels, backhoes, high towers, and other heavy equipment needed in a logging operation.
- **Log-chipper operators** run chippers that convert logs into wood chips.

Work Hazards and Conditions

Logging jobs are physically demanding. You must be willing to spend all your time outdoors, sometimes in poor weather and often in isolated areas. While most workers can return home every night, a few must live close to the job in bunkhouses. In the West, the commute to the job is often much longer than in other areas of the country.

Except those that are almost completely mechanized, logging jobs involve lifting, climbing, and other strenuous activities and carry some risk. Falling trees and branches are a constant threat, as are the dangers associated with handling logs and using sawing equipment. Slippery or muddy ground and hidden roots or vines reduce efficiency and present a constant danger, especially in the presence of moving vehicles and machinery. There is also the annoyance of coping with nature—poisonous plants, brambles, insects, snakes, heat, and humidity—as well as the loud noise of sawing and skidding operations. On the job, logging workers wear hard hats, eye and ear protection, and safety clothing and boots. Forest conservation jobs are usually much less hazardous.

On the Job with a Logging Crew

Since graduating from college with a bachelor's degree in forest management, Daniel Carpenter has worked in procurement—buying wood—for large and small companies and has also managed some logging operations. Daniel now works for a small wood-buying company, procuring pine and hardwood trees for seven crews to log and overseeing one crew. He makes sure the crew stays within the property boundaries and uses proper harvesting techniques to protect the environment. The contract crew he supervises is part of an operation owned by three family members who work on the crew.

Feller or Buncher Operator. One of the owners operates this machine. He is in his thirties and has been logging most of his life—just like the rest of his family. He has learned the profession on the job by operating a chain saw, loading trucks, and performing mechanical repairs.

Skidder Operator. This operator retrieves piles of logs, puts them through a delimbing gate, and then takes them to the landing area. This is an entry-level job that does not require experience. When the terrain requires the timber to be cut by chain saws, he fastens chokes around the logs so they can be dragged to the landing.

Knuckle-Boom Loader Operator. The loader is operated by the other owner. He sorts the logs so his company will receive the highest value for them. He also delimbs, if needed.

Chain Saw Workers. Another crew Daniel occasionally works with includes the same personnel plus another skidder operator and several workers who float among jobs to delimb logs with chain saws. When crews in his area work in the mountains, the job becomes more of a hard-hat operation: the trees are cut by chain saws, and then chokers or cables are fastened around them before they are skidded or pulled to the landing area.

Job Qualifications and Training

Little formal education is required in logging occupations. In the past, most logging workers learned their skills through on-the-job training, with instruction coming primarily from experienced workers. Logging has also tended to run in families, as parents pass their skills on to their children. Today, those who operate equipment, especially heavy machinery, still require some on-the-job training. However, it has also become common to take classes from trade associations and other industry groups to learn how to operate equipment and how to comply with environmental laws and safety regulations. Some programs lead to logger certification. In Canada, loggers may need heavy-equipment operations certification, air-brake certification, and Workplace Hazardous Materials Information Systems certification. Loggers may also need first aid certification and certification for logging-machine operation.

Quite often, experience in other occupations can lead to jobs in logging. For example, equipment operators, such as truck drivers and bulldozer and crane operators, can assume skidding and yarding functions.

Inexperienced loggers often begin as laborers. Those who have the motor skills required for the efficient use of power saws and other equipment may become fallers and buckers. Experience with logging operations may lead to jobs operating complicated machinery. Some loggers advance to crew supervisors, and some become contractors working with one or more crews.

Job Outlook and Earnings

The employment of logging workers is expected to decline despite a steady demand for lumber and other wood products. Logging crews continue to get smaller as mechanization reduces the number of workers required to complete a job. There will not be as great a need for fallers, buckers, choke setters, and others whose jobs are labor intensive. However, employment of machinery and equipment operators should not be as severely affected. Another reason for reduced employment is that less land is now available for logging due to conservation and environmental efforts, especially in federal forests in the West and Northwest.

Your earnings as a logger depend on where you work and the nature of your job. Workers in Alaska and the Northwest earn more than those in the South, where it is generally cheaper to live. The greater skill a job requires, the more you will earn. Entry-level jobs may pay minimum wage, while some experienced machinery operators earn more than $26 an hour. Canadian machinery operators earned an average of CAN$19.50 per hour.

Careers in the Forestry Industry

Foresters put on their hard hats to perform a variety of jobs. They may work for private companies as timber cruisers, spending their days in the woods to inventory the type, amount, and location of all standing timber. Later, they may supervise the removal of timber from the plot. Foresters also supervise tree planting and growth. Those who work for state and federal governments manage public forests and parks. In the course of a workday, foresters often walk miles, scramble over trees, wade through streams, and climb hills and mountains in all kinds of weather. Some even fight forest fires. Independent consultants and less-experienced foresters spend most of their time outdoors, overseeing or participating in hands-on work.

Job Qualifications and Training

The minimum educational requirement for a career as a forester is almost always a bachelor's degree in forestry, although, on occasion, the federal government allows applicants to substitute experience and appropriate education for this degree. Prospective foresters should attend a college with a program accredited by the Society of American Foresters. Besides scientific, technical, and forest management classes, many schools expect their students to complete a field session either in a camp operated by the school or in a cooperative work-study program. They also encourage all students to take summer jobs that give them experience in forestry or conservation work. To work as a forester in many states, you must acquire the designation Professional Forester, which is accomplished by meeting certain state licensing or registration requirements.

Job Outlook and Earnings

Employment of foresters will grow slowly over the next ten years. Job opportunities will be best with state and local governments. The reduction of timber harvesting on public lands in the Northwest and California will dampen job growth for private industry foresters in these areas. However, opportunities will be better for foresters in the Southeast because much of the forested land there is privately owned and less subject to conservation regulation. Still, a rising demand for timber has created a need for forest management plans that maximize production while sustaining the environment.

The average income for all foresters in the United States is more than $51,000 a year. In Canada, foresters earn about CAN$36,600 per year. The lowest 10 percent earns less than $34,000 in the United States and less than CAN$31,000 in Canada. The highest 10 percent earns about $75,000 in the United States and about CAN$53,000 in Canada. Starting salaries for jobs with the federal government and in private industry are slightly above those with state and local governments.

On the Job with a Forester

While she was in high school, Jennifer Carpenter went to the library to investigate careers. She decided that being a forester would be an excellent choice as it would take advantage of her interest in mathematics and science while letting her work outdoors. During college, Jennifer began to learn what a career as a forester would be like through her participation in a cooperative education program.

One semester, Jennifer worked as a research assistant for a large paper company. She worked in the company's greenhouse and in the forest measuring trees to see which of the trees with genetically controlled backgrounds were best to breed. In the woods, she always wore a bright orange hard hat to protect herself from falling limbs and make her more visible to hunters. She also faced the hazards of snakes and ticks.

In her second semester as a cooperative education student, Jennifer worked for the same company in the technical service department. She held an office job that gave her experience computer mapping property using a geographic information system (GIS). During her final semester with the company, Jennifer worked in the field office as a land-management technician. This time she worked outdoors cruising timber. She accomplished this by measuring every tree in quarter-acre plots placed systematically throughout the stand of timber in order to evaluate what wood products were available for harvesting. To do this job effectively, Jennifer had to follow a systematic grid to avoid missing any plots, so she was forced to cross many creeks. The work conditions were challenging—temperatures often exceeded ninety degrees, and it rained often. Another work assignment required her to manage controlled burns to prepare land for replanting.

Working as a Resource Forester. After graduation with her bachelor's degree in forest management, Jennifer accepted a job with a paper company as a resource forester working outdoor jobs. One of her responsibilities involved managing several areas of the company's land. She helped with prescribed burning, timber inventory, road layout, herbicide use, supervision of tree planters, and hiring of contractors. Another part of her job was to find and buy timber from private landowners. She especially enjoyed working outside on spring days.

Jennifer received a promotion to the company's regional office to work on the technical side of forestry, installing and implementing a GIS system. She collected information from foresters in the field to use in strategic planning. Recently, she moved to another part of the state and took a job as coordinator of forest information systems for a consulting company. In the future, Jennifer may return to wearing a hard hat on a daily basis by starting her own business, since there are many exciting opportunities for small consulting firms.

Lumberjack Competitions. Jennifer began competing in lumberjack competitions when she was in a forestry club in college and still enjoys them. Many people in logging and forestry occupations compete in events such as single bucking and crosscutting (bucking with a partner), speed chopping, and log burling (spinning a log until one competitor falls off). Attending one of these events may give you the opportunity to talk with a competitor and learn more about a career in logging or forestry. You will also get to see old-time logging tools being used.

Career Advice. Jennifer recommends that future foresters take part in a cooperative education program. Participating in such a program can help you determine whether a career in forestry is for you, and it will help you decide what specific area of forestry most appeals to you.

Forestry Technicians
Forestry technicians work under the supervision of foresters. Like foresters, they work for local, state, and federal governments and

private companies. Most of these jobs are outdoors and require a hard hat at all times. As a forestry technician, you could be part of a team measuring and evaluating trees, marking trees for sale, planting new trees, and building roads in forests. You could even find yourself operating bulldozers and other pieces of heavy equipment. If you work for a government unit, you are most likely to assist forest rangers or help with fighting fires. With experience as a technician, you could advance to supervisory positions, and, with additional schooling, you could become a forester.

Education. To become a forestry technician, you should complete a two-year program in forestry at a community college or technical school. Working as a forestry aide may also give you the necessary skills.

Earnings. What you earn as a forest technician varies across the country and across employers. The highest-paying jobs are in the West. If you work for a private company, you will be paid by the hour, while a job with the government will pay you a set salary. Your earnings will be based on experience and could vary from about $14,400 a year to more than $36,000 a year.

Careers Working in a Sawmill

Working in a sawmill is really an assembly-line job. Logs come in one end, and lumber comes out the other—whether you are working in a small mill with just a few employees or a large one with hundreds. No matter what your job, you will wear a hard hat and most likely ear and eye protection as well. There are no special educational requirements for becoming a sawmill worker, but mills prefer to hire high school graduates. You will learn through on-the-job training, starting in a job that requires considerable handling of lumber. Through observation, you will learn to operate some of the complex equipment. For some positions, industry and trade associations offer additional training. Log mill workers can expect to take even more classes in the future as mills increasingly use laser and computer technology. Advancement can also include supervisory positions. Here is an overview of some of the jobs in a sawmill:

- **Yard workers** drive loaders to stack logs as they come into the mill. Few logs are now stored in ponds. A scaler takes inventory of the logs, and loader drivers take the logs to the mill.
- **Debarker operators** run a machine that does exactly what the name implies—it removes bark from logs. It is operated by a worker who sits in a cab manipulating various controls.
- **Head sawyers** have the most important job in the mill. They use computers to help determine how to cut each log into boards. The value of a log can vary greatly depending on the way it is initially cut.
- **Edger operators** trim the rough edges from boards and make the sides straight and even. Operators use computers in making their decisions on how to edge a board properly.
- **Trimmer operators** remove knots and other defects and cut the logs into lengths.
- **Graders** code wood according to its characteristics so it can be sorted for appropriate use. Graders usually go to school for two to three weeks to learn about grading.
- **Green-chain workers** are entry-level workers who take lumber coded by the grader off the line and place it in the right spot.
- **Kiln operators** adjust knobs and dials to get the right amount of steam and heat in a kiln to dry lumber. This is a skilled position.
- **Planers** operate machines that smooth the logs once they are dry. This can be an apprentice position.

- **Filers** keep the saws sharp. Filers learn this job through apprenticeships.
- **Maintenance workers** keep the plant and its machinery functioning.

Job Outlook and Earnings

The greater the need for lumber and wood products, the more jobs there are in sawmills, plywood and veneer factories, and paper mills. New technology and increasing mechanization may reduce job opportunities. However, many exciting jobs are on the horizon as lasers, scanners, and computers are being introduced to the industry. Sawmill workers earn an average of $27,300 per year.

For More Information

For information about logging careers, contact the school of forestry at your state land-grant college or one of the following:

American Forest & Paper Association
1111 Nineteenth Street NW, Suite 800
Washington, DC 20036
www.afandpa.org

American Loggers Council
PO Box 966
Hemphill, TX 75948
www.americanloggers.org

Canadian Lumbermen's Association
30 Concourse Gate, Suite 200
Ottawa, ON K2E 7V7
Canada
www.canadianlumbermen.com

Great Lakes Timber Professionals Association
3243 Golf Course Road
PO Box 1278
Rhinelander, WI 54501
www.timberpa.com

National Hardwood Lumber Association
6830 Raleigh LaGrange Road
Memphis, TN 38134
www.natlhardwood.org

Northeastern Loggers' Association
3311 State Route 28
PO Box 69
Old Forge, NY 13420
www.northernlogger.com

For information about the forestry profession and lists of schools offering education in forestry, send a self-addressed, stamped business envelope to:

Canadian Forestry Association
1027 Pembroke Street East
Pembroke, ON K8A 3M4
Canada
www.canadianforestry.com

Society of American Foresters
5400 Grosvenor Lane
Bethesda, MD 20814
www.safnet.org

CHAPTER SEVEN

Jobs in the Petroleum Industry

Petroleum is one of the world's most valuable natural resources. In 2006, three U.S. oil companies announced they had discovered the largest oil find in a generation. Up to fifteen billion barrels of oils were found more than thirty thousand feet below the surface of the Gulf of Mexico. Canada plans to double its oil production by the year 2020. Petroleum, which includes oil and natural gas, powers our cars, sends planes streaking around the world, heats homes, and provides the power for trains, boats, and tractors. Petroleum is also part of products that we use every day, such as plastics, drugs, detergents, chemicals, fertilizers, synthetic rubber, and paint.

If you decide to work in the petroleum industry, you will have a choice of working in several areas:

- **Exploration** involves searching for geologic formations that are likely to contain oil and gas.
- **Drilling** involves extracting oil and gas from beneath the ground or sea and maintaining wells.
- **Refining** involves refining crude oil and gas into products that we can use.

No matter which area you choose, the majority of jobs directly involved with oil and gas will require you to wear a hard hat.

Careers in Exploring for Oil

Oil is found throughout the world in all sorts of places—from deserts to swamps to forests to mountains and even under the ocean floor. Small crews of specialized workers explore for oil and gas deposits by studying and mapping the subsurface of the land or ocean. They use sophisticated equipment, including computers and remote-sensing satellites. They also collect and analyze samples of rock, clay, and sand found in different layers of the earth. These small exploration teams are usually headed by geologists or geophysicists who interpret all of the data gathered.

Other specialists who may be part of these teams include:

- **Paleontologists**, who study fossil remains to find oil
- **Mineralogists**, who study mineral and rock samples
- **Oceanographers**, who study oceans and coastal waters
- **Stratigraphers**, who look at rock layers to find the ones likely to have oil and gas
- **Photogeologists**, who interpret aerial photographs

To enter each of these professions, a bachelor's degree is a necessity; however, better jobs with good advancement potential usually require a master's degree.

Petroleum technicians are also important members of exploration teams. They collect and examine geological data and test geological samples to determine petroleum and mineral content. While some technicians have bachelor's degrees, most have an associate's degree from a community or technical college. They usually begin their careers in the petroleum industry by working as trainees in routine positions under the supervision of professional members of the team or experienced technicians. Exploration teams may also have surveyors, surveying technicians, and drafters who survey and map potential oil fields.

Members of exploration teams must have the physical stamina to work in every type of terrain and climate. Besides strong computer skills, they need good interpersonal skills and strong oral and written communication skills to communicate their findings. They must also be willing to travel because the best exploration opportunities are in other countries, where, unlike in the United States, many of the most likely petroleum-producing areas have yet to be explored. However, the implementation of new technologies that expand drilling possibilities and improve the performance of reservoirs in the United States and the Gulf of Mexico may create new opportunities in this country.

Job Outlook and Earnings

If you decide to work in this area of the petroleum industry, you should understand that employment is cyclical and largely affected by the price of oil and gas. When prices are low, oil and gas producers curtail exploration, and workers on exploration teams are laid off. When prices are up, companies have the money to renew exploration and hire workers in large numbers. Salaries for geologists, geophysicists, and oceanographers in the United States average more than $72,600 a year, and in Canada the average salary is CAN$60,000 a year. The middle 50 percent earns between $51,800 and $100,600. The highest 10 percent earns nearly $136,000, while the lowest 10 percent earns $39,700. Technicians receive an average hourly wage of about $22.

On the Job with an Exploration Team

Roy Smith has worked in just about every area of the petroleum industry, from exploring for oil to drilling and refining. His introduction to the petroleum industry came shortly after he graduated from high school and went to work on an exploration team as a shooter's helper. The shooter crew's work began after geologists had selected an area they wanted to investigate more closely for oil. Surveyors had set out a pattern of places to drill holes eight to ten miles long and about one-quarter mile wide. Two drilling crews, each with a truck and drilling rig, had dug holes approximately sixty feet deep. It was Roy's job to help lower dynamite into the holes to the depth prescribed by the experts in the seismograph truck, who would also tell the crew by radio when to shoot the charge. The seismograph truck had equipment to measure the shock waves from the dynamite blast to get what could be called a photograph of the geological formations. After the blast, Roy's crew returned to the hole and pulled out the wire before going to the next hole. Although Roy worked in exploration quite awhile ago, the process remains the same, except that today's equipment is more sophisticated.

Careers in Drilling for Oil

Once an exploratory team has determined that a site may contain oil or gas, the drilling team takes over. The team works under the direction of petroleum engineers. First, the team sinks test wells to determine if a site actually contains oil or gas. The initial drilling is often unsuccessful. If oil or gas is discovered, more wells are drilled, and the field is developed.

Work Hazards and Conditions

Oil drilling can be hazardous work that includes the possibility of oil spills, fires, and other kinds of accidents. Objects may fall as the pipe is run in and out of the well, and the work involves considerable lifting and working with oily tools. Still, the rate of work-related accidents is actually lower in the petroleum industry than that for the entire private sector.

If you choose to work on a drilling team, your job is most likely to be in Texas, Louisiana, Oklahoma, California, Colorado, or Alaska because most of the oil and gas in the United States are located in these states. Also, you can expect to work shifts because drilling operations never stop. On land, drilling teams work six days, eight hours a day, before they have time off. On offshore rigs, drilling team members may stay on the rigs for two weeks at a time and work much longer days.

Petroleum Engineers

Extracting oil from the ground in the most efficient and profitable way is the task of petroleum engineers. They begin by working with exploration team specialists to understand the geologic formation and properties of rock containing the reservoir. Then the engineers determine the drilling methods to be used and monitor the actual drilling. Because only a small proportion of oil and gas in a reservoir will flow out under natural forces, petroleum engineers develop and use various enhanced-recovery methods to force more oil out. When the drilling is completed, they supervise the operation of the well and maintenance of the equipment. Beginning petroleum engineers work under the supervision of experienced engineers as they learn their jobs.

Job Qualifications and Training

A bachelor's degree is generally required for entry-level jobs. Because only a few schools offer degrees in petroleum engineering, college graduates can qualify for jobs with degrees in geology or civil, mechanical, or mining engineering that include course work in petroleum engineering. Many job applicants also earn master's degrees. In addition, large companies have formal training programs. For many jobs, you will need to become a licensed engineer. You can begin this process by taking the initial test after graduation and then a second test after you have suitable work experience.

Job Outlook and Earnings

Jobs for petroleum engineers are expected to grow slowly over the next ten years. This may change as companies invest more in oil and gas exploration if oil and gas prices remain high. The best opportunities for petroleum engineers may be in other countries that are expanding oil exploration. The average annual salary for petroleum engineers is $98,300, with the middle 50 percent earning between $75,800 and $123,000. The lowest 10 percent earns $58,000 per year, while the highest 10 percent earns over $145,600.

On the Job with a Petroleum Engineer

While attending college for his bachelor's degree in petroleum engineering, Emanuel Guidry spent three summers working in oil fields garnering considerable knowledge of the petroleum industry. During the first summer, he put on a hard hat and steel-toed shoes to perform hard physical labor for a service company. Under the direction of an operator, he lowered wire lines with tools on them into wells. The different tools were used to take pressure and temperature readings and samples of fluids, sand, mud, and water in the wells. At times, he and the operator would treat wells to increase production.

Emanuel became an operator and worked at this job for two summers, handling more responsibilities the second summer, when he became an engineering intern at an oil and gas company and assisted a petroleum engineer in charge of several wells. He helped the engineer monitor production from the wells, planned work to increase production, and made sure the wells complied with state and federal regulations. Emanuel continued to work in this job part-time during his final year in college.

After graduation, Emanuel took a one-year training position as a development engineer at the company where he completed his internship. In the petroleum industry, as in others, an internship can lead to a job after graduation for those who excel. Emanuel's job involved work similar to what he had performed as an intern. In addition, he monitored costs, an important task as the cost of producing oil should not exceed the amount the oil company receives for the product.

Climbing the Career Ladder at an Oil Company. How fast you climb the career ladder depends to some degree on the cyclical nature of this industry. When production slows, so do opportunities for advancement. It also takes time to gain experience. After his year as a development engineer, Emanuel worked in reservoir engineering to focus on finding reserves and conducting drilling engineering work. He then became a supervisor of a group of ten to twelve engineers who worked in oil fields in different areas. This job required considerable traveling and meant spending more time in the office. Emanuel was responsible for the engineers' training and career development and helped them set career goals, evaluated job performance, and counseled them. The next step for Emanuel was to become a director and have the responsibility of managing supervisors from several areas, such as production, regulations, and safety. He then became an area manager reporting to a regional manager.

Not all engineers want to follow Emanuel's career route, in which he now spends most of his time in an office. Many elect to remain out in the field, wearing hard hats in a variety of exploration, drilling, and production jobs.

Career Advice. Emanuel believes it is important to find out what you enjoy doing and fit it into a career. He has always been interested in his work because he is doing what he enjoys. Emanuel also advises prospective engineers to be patient and to realize that they may not get the job they want right away. In your career, he believes that it is important both to set lofty, long-term goals and smaller, short-term ones. Finally, he counsels you not to be afraid to help someone else achieve.

Technicians and Laborers

Workers with a wide variety of skills are needed to get oil from the ground. In the past, you could put on a hard hat and start as a roustabout, picking up different skills through on-the-job training. Because of technological advances, more education is needed, and a new class of worker, called a technician, has emerged. While it is possible to get a job as a high school graduate, many technicians have attended two-year technical and community colleges to meet the challenge of newer methods of drilling for oil. A few technician jobs require workers to have bachelor's degrees. You will find schools offering technician training primarily in the West and Southwest, where most oil and gas fields are located. Here is an overview of some of the jobs you might hold as a petroleum technician:

- **Tool pushers** are in charge of one or more drilling rigs. They oversee every aspect of drilling, from setting up the rigs to selecting drill bits to arranging for the delivery of all tools and supplies.
- **Rotary drillers** use a rotating drill bit attached to a pipe to bore holes in the ground. As the hole gets deeper, more pipe is added. When the drill bit becomes dull, the drill bit and all the pipe must be hauled to the surface so the drill bit can be replaced. Rotary drillers supervise crews of four or five workers (rotary-driller helpers) and operate machines that control the speed of the drill and the weight on the bit. They also keep a record of the types of strata that have been drilled through each day.
- **Derrick operators** are second in charge of rotary drilling crews and work on a small platform high up on the rig. They help run the pipe in and out of the hole and operate the pumps that circulate the mud through the pipe to keep the drill bit cool. In addition, they mix the drilling mud.
- **Engine operators** are in charge of the operation and maintenance of the engines that provide power for drilling and hoisting.
- **Cementers** mix cement and pump it into the space between the casing and well wall to prevent any cave-ins.
- **Roustabouts** are the laborers in the oil fields. This is an entry-level job in which training is received from more experienced workers. What roustabouts do varies from job to job. Some are rotary-driller helpers, guiding the lower

ends of pipe to well openings and connecting pipe joints and drill bits. Others drive trucks, repair machinery, perform maintenance and cleanup work, and do whatever else their supervisors ask them to do.

- **Welders, pipe fitters, electricians, and machinists** are among the other skilled workers who are employed during drilling and when the well is operating. On offshore drilling operations, additional workers are needed, including cooks, radio operators, crews to operate boats and barges, and helicopter pilots.

On the Job on a Drilling Rig

After a stint in the military, Roy Smith—whose work as a shooter's helper was described earlier in the chapter—returned to the petroleum industry to work on a drilling rig. He started on the graveyard shift in an entry-level job. Roy and another worker connected pieces of pipe together as the well was drilled deeper. The two workers also broke the pipe apart as it was removed from the well to put on new drill bits. This was a difficult and dirty job as falling mud, dirt, and rock were always an issue.

Even if you start at the bottom, it is possible to climb the career ladder on well-drilling rigs. One day, the driller who ran Roy's shift asked him if he could handle operating a derrick. Roy's job training consisted of working for four hours with the derrick operator on the evening shift. The first few weeks were frightening until he became used to working on a platform sixty feet in the air, and Roy admits to fastening his seat belt very tightly. He only worked on the derrick platform when pipe was run in and out of the well. He spent the rest of his time making sure the drilling mud was mixed correctly.

Job Outlook and Earnings

Oil companies in the United States and Canada are investing more money into exploration because oil and gas prices are high. As long as the prices remain high, exploration will grow. A decline in prices means a decline in the number of workers needed to drill and operate wells, which also limits opportunities for advancement. Most new jobs will still come through the replacement of workers who retire or transfer to other industries. Workers with the best opportunities are those with strong technical skills and considerable experience in the industry.

The average earnings of nonsupervisory workers in the petroleum industry are significantly higher than for those in private industry. Rotary drill operators earn more than $19 per hour, while derrick operators earn nearly $16. Roustabouts earn close to $13 per hour.

Careers in Refining Oil

The crude oil that flows out of wells has little use before it is processed. It is transported to refineries by trucks, railroad tank cars, pipelines, and tankers, where it is turned into gasoline, diesel oil, lubricating oil, asphalt, and petrochemicals used in thousands of products, from plastics to cosmetics. Refineries are easy to recognize as they are filled with tanks, towers, and miles of pipeline. When the crude oil arrives in the refinery, it is stored in tanks. Then it is pumped through the plant, and different processes change it into the products that we use.

Most refineries are located close to oil fields, cities, or ports. The more than 150 refineries in the United States vary from plants that employ only a few workers to those with thousands. If you choose to be one of the more than one hundred thousand people working in refineries, you will find a job in one of these three main areas: operations, maintenance, or engineering.

Operations Workers

Refining oil has become a very mechanized operation. Operators monitor and direct the continuous operation of petroleum refining and processing units from rooms with automatic controls.

They operate controls to regulate temperature, pressure, rate of flow, and tank level in petroleum refining units according to processing schedules. Being an operator is only a hard-hat job when the operator walks around the plant to detect problems such as leaks and equipment malfunctions. These problems are reported to the refinery engineers. Because refineries run twenty-four-hour days throughout the year, operators work shifts, weekends, and some holidays.

To obtain a job as an operator, you will need to be a high school graduate. Many operators also have some training from community or technical colleges. In this job, you start as a junior operator of a single unit in the refinery. As you gain experience, you can advance to operator of a unit and then to stillman (the manager of a unit).

Maintenance Workers

More than half of all employees at refineries are maintenance workers. They must keep all the refinery equipment running smoothly through repair and maintenance work. Another part of this job is inspecting the tanks, pipes, pipe fittings, towers, and pumps for leaks.

While maintenance workers can learn their skills on the job, they increasingly have additional technical training, and some participate in apprenticeship programs. Included in the maintenance area are jobs for welders, mechanics, machinists, and electricians. Promotion is a strong possibility. For example, an entry-level worker could move to mechanic to assistant supervisor to maintenance mechanic superintendent.

Engineers

Most engineers who work at refineries are chemical engineers, although there are some jobs for mechanical engineers. The engineers who work directly for the refinery are responsible for keeping the operation running. They are in charge of monitoring and improving the operation, upgrading the equipment, and overseeing the repair work. Engineers employed by outside engineering firms have the job of finding new ways to improve the quality of petroleum products and the production of these products. They also design new refineries and the expansion of existing refineries.

You need at least a bachelor's degree in chemical engineering. You will start as a junior engineer who reports to a senior engineer, learning on the job as you become familiar with refinery operations. You may also learn by using computer simulation programs. After several years, you may advance to senior engineer responsible for one or more units of the refinery, then to supervisor of a refinery section made up of several units. You can then advance to engineering manager of an entire project or to department manager with an engineering company or to refinery manager if you work for the refining company.

Engineering Technicians

The chemical engineering technicians at refineries work for the engineers. They run tests for them in laboratories, help them monitor refinery operations, and assist with other jobs as needed. These technicians need to have completed a two-year community or technical college program. Some have earned bachelor's degrees.

On the Job in Maintenance and Operations

After working in exploration and drilling, Roy Smith switched to working at a refinery that was small when he started. Over the years, different units were added until it became a large refinery producing a wide variety of products, from gasoline to plastics. Before he left this company, Roy had worked in maintenance and operations and was steadily promoted from entry-level general maintenance helper to stillman, which is the top nonmanagement job in the refinery.

General Maintenance Helper. In this job, Roy never knew where he would be working from one day to the next. Each morning he was assigned to a crafts worker, such as a welder, pipe fitter, equipment operator, mechanic, or boilermaker. He performed manual labor that required him to follow the crafts worker's instructions. This was not an easy job as he could be carrying heavy tools or cleaning heat exchangers. Most of his work was out in the refinery.

The longer Roy worked in this job, the more he learned about the different crafts. After working as a helper for two years, he successfully applied for a job as an equipment operator. He started out as a pickup truck driver, delivering workers and tools to different sites at the refinery, then he advanced to a position as light-truck driver.

A Stint in the Laboratory. When a recession struck the refining industry, Roy had the choice of being laid off or returning to his first job as a general maintenance helper. He chose maintenance and then moved to a job as a laboratory helper, where he worked a rotating shift. Roy started the shift outside, collecting samples from the tanks. Then he ran tests on the samples until the end of his shift. After a couple of years, the economy improved, and Roy had the opportunity to transfer to operations.

Working in Operations. Roy moved into the stills group, which operates the individual units making up the refinery. Each unit was headed by a stillman who managed five operators who, in turn, handled different operations within the unit. Roy became an operator helper. In one task, he tested the water in cooling towers and added chemicals to keep it appropriately balanced. In another, he helped operators place equipment in and out of service, which included finding leaks and getting equipment ready for maintenance.

The next step up the career ladder for Roy was to senior operator helper in a unit. This was his opportunity to learn how to be an operator. It was an indoor job, although he walked through the unit several times a day with the operator to check for leaks and become familiar with the equipment.

From helper, Roy became a vacation operator, which required him to learn thirty different operator jobs. Because he had already worked in maintenance and with several operators as a helper, he had a good idea of how the refinery worked. As an operator, Roy used computers to monitor continuously what happened in the refinery, and he kept his equipment operating within the parameters set by the stillman. Whenever he had a question, the stillman was always there to help him. The longer Roy worked as an operator, the more he could work as a vacation replacement for the stillman. With all this experience, Roy was promoted to stillman.

Job Outlook and Earnings

Although there are not nearly as many refineries in the United States as there were twenty years ago, demand for refinery workers is holding steady because of the continuing need to refine oil for gasoline and other petroleum and petrochemical products. Automation has reduced the demand for operations workers, but there is an ongoing need for maintenance and engineering personnel.

The highest-paid employees in refineries are the chemical engineers. The average annual salary for engineers is more than $59,000 per year in the United States. Canadian engineers earn about CAN$63,000 per year. Workers in operations and maintenance are generally members of unions who receive good benefits as well as wages higher than the average for all industries.

For More Information

You can find information on training and career opportunities for geologists and petroleum engineers by contacting:

American Petroleum Institute
1220 L Street NW
Washington, DC 20005
www.api.org

Canadian Association of Petroleum Producers
350 Seventh Avenue SW, Suite 2100
Calgary, AL T2P 3N9
Canada
www.capp.ca

Society of Petroleum Engineers
PO Box 833836
Richardson, TX 75083
www.spe.org

High school students can find out more about careers as petroleum engineers by contacting the resources listed for civil engineers at the end of Chapter 2.

To learn more about careers with an oil company, write:

Exxon Mobil Corporation
U.S. Recruiting & Employment
PO Box 2180
Houston, TX 77252
www.exxon.mobil.com

Phillips Petroleum
Employment & College Relations
PO Box 1267
Ponca City, OK 74602
www.phillips66.com

CHAPTER EIGHT

Jobs in the Utility Sector

lip a switch and the lights come on. Turn on the kitchen faucet and get water to drink. Turn up the thermostat and your home gets warm. Turn on the television and watch your favorite show. These are all simple acts for us. But getting each of these services into our homes requires complex systems that are installed, monitored, and maintained by many workers who are wearing their hard hats.

People depend so much on the services that utility companies provide that they are considered "public goods" and are heavily regulated. In the past, many utilities were actually monopolies in their service areas. However, in order to promote efficiency, lower costs to customers, and increase service options, legislation is increasingly introducing competition to the utilities arena. For example, in many areas you now can buy electricity or telephone service from more than one company.

Where electric, water supply, sanitary services, and gas utilities companies are located determines their size and ownership. In urban areas, these utilities are generally large, privately owned companies. In rural areas and small towns, utilities are usually funded and operated by state or local government or citizen groups because the customer base is too small to pay for building plants. Large telecommunications companies typically offer services across state lines, although there are some small companies offering service to a limited area.

Work Hazards and Conditions

Because utility services are produced and used continuously throughout the day, utility employees often work split, weekend, and night shifts. The average workweek is more than forty hours—higher than the average for all industries because utility employees often must work overtime and irregular hours to accommodate peaks in demand and to repair damage caused by storms, cold weather, and accidents. To offer consistent service to customers, maintenance and repair workers may have to remain on call twenty-four hours a day to handle emergencies.

Depending on the job, work conditions vary for utility workers. They may work in dusty and dirty areas and very hot or cold weather. Sometimes they work in confined areas, ditches, and tunnels; under houses and streets; up on ladders and scaffolds and other high spots; or in other uncomfortable places. Utility workers might risk injury from electrical shock, falls, and cuts, and they must follow strict safety procedures. To decrease the risk of injury, the law requires them to wear protective gear such as hard hats, safety belts, boots, and glasses.

Careers in Electric, Water, Sanitary Services, and Gas Utilities

More than 549,000 workers are employed in nongovernment public utilities that provide electricity, gas, water, and sanitary services. More than 70 percent of these jobs are with electric utilities, approximately 19 percent with gas companies, and almost 8 percent with water supply and sanitary services. Almost half of the workers employed at these public utilities work in precision production or operator, fabricator, or laborer occupations.

Careers in Electric Services

Our daily routines revolve around electricity. Whenever you turn on a light, watch television, or browse the Internet, you enjoy the benefits of electricity. When a cashier rings up a bill or you relax under an electric blanket, you use electricity. Getting that electricity into our homes, schools, and workplaces requires skilled trade workers. Some of these workers install networks of wires to bring electricity from generating plants to customers. They also maintain and repair these lines.

Power-Line Workers

About one-third of the utility installers and repairers are employed as electrical power-line workers. As a line installer, you would be responsible for installing power lines that bring electricity from power plants to substations, where the voltage is reduced, and then to customers. Line installers begin the construction of new lines by erecting the poles or towers required to carry the wires. After the poles are in place, the installers—wearing their protective hard hats, gloves, and safety belts—climb the poles to string the wires. They also install underground power lines and set up service for customers.

Entry-level installers may be hired as ground workers, helpers, or tree trimmers who clear branches from power lines. These workers may advance to positions where they string wires and perform service installations. With experience, they may advance to more sophisticated maintenance and repair positions.

When wires break or poles are knocked down, power-line workers must make emergency repairs. They are also responsible for performing routine inspections and making necessary repairs and changes to prevent larger problems in the future.

Additional Jobs

Within power plants that generate electricity, there are many hard-hat jobs, especially in repair and maintenance. The mechanical components of generators, plant piping, water inlets, steam boilers, pumps, and other equipment must be kept in excellent condition. Specialty jobs in repair and maintenance include pipe fitter, electrician, welder, boilermaker, and carpenter. Electric utility plants also employ operators, who spend most of their time in special rooms to control and operate machinery.

On the Job at a Small Utility Company

Bob Sessions has worked as a repairer for a small electric utility for many years. When he started his career, it was customary to learn through on-the-job training. However, he now recommends taking classes through local junior colleges or gaining experience through an apprenticeship. As a repairer, Bob restores electrical power to homes and businesses. He believes good people skills are important because he is in contact with so many customers each day.

Bob constantly faces new challenges in his work. When he goes to a site, he never knows exactly what he will find. He must analyze a situation from all angles to discover the problem and determine exactly how to reconnect power to the customer. Much of his workday is spent in a bucket truck repairing lines high in the air.

Bob's job is both stressful and fast paced. At any time during the day or night, he may have to rush to handle an emergency electrical outage because customers want their service restored promptly. He also has to work quickly and efficiently to meet deadlines.

On the Job in Utilities Operations

Bob Ergeberg doesn't work for a utility company. Instead, he maintains all of the electrical power, air-conditioning, heating, and fire protection systems at a university. With almost sixty-five hundred people on the campus, he always has something for his twenty-seven employees to fix. Bob must know and enforce all of the safety rules that his hard-hat workers must follow. In addition, he must understand every aspect of all the utility company products used on campus, from the electricity that powers air conditioners to the water everyone drinks.

One of Bob's employees is Leroy Neilson, a maintenance foreman. After a fulfilling career in the U.S. Navy as a boiler technician on an aircraft carrier, Leroy moved into general utility maintenance.

Most of the skills Leroy uses were learned on the job, but his mechanical aptitude helped him get started. Leroy has also used his basic knowledge of electricity and science in working with the electrical wiring and temperature and pressure units on heating, cooling, and refrigerating equipment. Leroy considers an ability to be a good troubleshooter essential because problems are not always apparent.

After Leroy has assigned his team members the work that needs to be accomplished, he often helps them with their jobs. He also frequently works alone because of the nature of many of the tasks. While Leroy likes the challenges that different jobs bring, he does not appreciate the heat of the machines, especially on hot summer days.

Careers in Gas Services

Gas is an important fuel. We use it to heat our homes, offices, and factories; cook meals; dry laundry; heat water; and power machinery. Natural gas is found underground and transported to gas companies throughout the country in pressurized pipelines. The utilities depressurize the gas, add its distinctive odor, and distribute it to customers. Many diverse jobs exist for those involved in the installation, maintenance, and repair of gas lines. It is highly possible to enter this industry as a laborer and advance as you gain skills on the job.

Careers in Water Supply Services

Water utilities provide, on average, more than 175 gallons a day of fresh, treated water daily to every United States resident. This adds up to more than forty billion gallons per day! This water comes from rivers, lakes, and wells and is filtered and treated by water supply services before being sold for residential, industrial, commercial, and public use.

Water-Treatment Technicians

To make sure that water is safe for people to drink and use for cooking, water-treatment technicians conduct tests to discover what chemicals it contains. They also help discover the best processes to remove contaminants from the water. Technicians may assist with any of the following processes: collecting water samples, conducting laboratory tests, and maintaining and making minor repairs on valves, pumps, and other equipment. Because water is located almost everywhere, water-treatment technicians may work in all types of environments.

Because of the dangerous chemicals that technicians use when testing water, they must be extremely careful. Protective gloves and hard hats are required when they work on water towers or in plants where contact with chemicals is possible. Technicians or other workers also use safety equipment when they repair and maintain plants and pipelines as well as when they install new water lines.

Careers in Sanitary Services

Sink water is awfully dirty after you wash all the dinner plates. Industrial wastewater is even dirtier and can contain many toxic chemicals. Sewage systems are set up to collect this water and treat it to make it safe to return to rivers, lakes, ponds, and the ocean.

Wastewater treatment plants are similar to water treatment plants, but the treatment processes and regulatory requirements are generally more complicated, especially for treating industrial waste.

With the growing number of people in society, the demand for clean water increases, yet at the same time more waste is being created. Sanitary service careers are involved not just with sewage systems, but also with the collection and disposal of all the garbage accumulated throughout the country every day. Hard-hat jobs are available for those involved in maintenance, repair, and operation of sewage plants and their pipelines and for those working at landfills, recycling plants, and incinerators.

Sanitary Engineers

Sanitary engineers help control and prevent pollution of water through designing, constructing, and supervising programs to improve the quality of wastewater. Some engineers design systems for filtering waste prior to its entry into lakes and rivers, and others test for and control radioactive pollution from industrial plants and laboratories. Due to the diversity of environmental problems, engineers often choose to specialize in one area of the field. For example, if you enjoy being outdoors, you may want to specialize in water resources. Through taking samples from bodies of water and testing them for harmful bacteria, engineers can find out what is polluting the water and devise ways to purify it.

Sewer Inspectors

Beneath our cities are miles of sewer lines that must be inspected for damage or defects. Most new lines can be inspected by robots carrying cameras. Older lines, though, can only be inspected by people looking for cracks and other defects. These inspectors work in pairs, each wearing hard hats with lights, rubber boots, surgical masks, and gloves and carrying gear to check for toxic gases. When they find a defect, its location is written in a notebook, it is marked with spray, and it may be photographed.

The conditions in sewers are not pleasant, and many people are reluctant to do this job. There is sewage, of course, and probably insects and unfriendly rats, and space is cramped. Those who work as inspectors choose it because it pays far better than most jobs.

Careers in Telecommunications

Millions of miles of wires and cables snake across the United States, giving us telephone, television, Internet, and other services. While providing telephone service still is the major focus of telephone companies, they are now expanding their services to transmit data, television, and other electronic products. Cable companies, too, have gone beyond their original missions to offer telephone service, Internet access, and other services. Because of the rapid explosion in communication, both telephone and cable companies are quickly expanding their networks by laying additional fiber-optic cable, which permits faster and higher-capacity transmissions than traditional copper wires. In addition, wireless telecommunications services for beepers, pagers, and cell and satellite phones are rapidly expanding.

Most of the more than one million jobs in the telecommunications industry are with telephone companies, typically large establishments with more than fifty employees. While you can find a job in almost every community, you are more likely to be employed in large cities.

Line Installation and Repair Workers

The principal jobs for hard-hat wearers in telecommunications are in line installation and repair, including maintenance. Close to two hundred thousand jobs exist in these areas. These jobs are similar to those for electric utilities, and the working conditions are almost the same—except telecommunications workers don't usually climb tall poles or towers, as these lines are usually underground.

While you can learn how to install or repair lines and cables through several years of on-the-job training, equipment manufacturers, schools, and industry organizations also offer training. For example, the Society of Cable Telecommunications Engineers provides certification programs for line installers and repairers. Applicants for this certification must be employed in the cable television industry and attend training at local chapters.

On the Job in Telecommunications

Phil Speidel started his work career as a house carpenter, but he needed another career when construction declined. While talking to his neighbor, who was in the cable industry, Phil discovered that many of his carpentry skills would serve him well in this field. So Phil entered the telecommunications industry as an installer for a local cable company.

Phil's Career Path. For four years, his primary responsibilities as an installer included connecting, disconnecting, installing, and repairing various cable wires. After he had learned the skills of an installer, Phil moved up to crew chief, where he supervised twelve installers. Every morning, Phil made sure that work and tools were ready for his crew. He would then briefly update crew members about their jobs for the day. During the day, Phil completed special tasks, monitored the progress of his crew members, and organized work for the next day. When one of his installers was behind on a project, Phil often assisted with the job. At night, once all the installers had finished, he locked all the company service trucks and closed the building.

After four years as a crew chief, Phil made a lateral move to the position of auditor. In this job, he monitored the quality of the service the cable company provided. Through frequent quality-control checks, Phil made sure the installers provided customers with the best service possible. After two years as an auditor, Phil earned a promotion to service technician. First, though, he had to complete a six-month correspondence course to gain the electrical knowledge required for this new position. As a service technician, Phil focused most of his time on troubleshooting as he tried to find out what caused system problems in the area from the main junction to the house connection.

His next step up to his present job as systems technician required both a practical application class and a safety class, and he had to score 100 percent to pass. In a practical application class, an instructor visits the job site to watch you complete a task using the skills you learned in class. In his present job, Phil is responsible for troubleshooting system problems and fixing them along the entire wire connection. This can mean finding a buried cable wire or finding out why there was an outage in service and fixing the problem.

Once Phil has been a systems technician for at least two years and has completed another certification, he will be ready to advance even higher. The next steps in his path have the potential of leading to a supervisory or management position.

Working Conditions at a Cable Company. Phil now works a ten-day shift and is the primary person on call every few days. He dislikes this work schedule, but he understands the importance of providing round-the-clock service to his customers. Because no one knows where a problem will occur in the cable line, Phil spends most of his time in a service van, driving to various locations in search of a system problem. For most of his jobs with this cable company, Phil has worked alone. The only time he has seen his supervisors is in the morning before leaving the office or in the evening when returning.

On-the-Job Safety. Phil stresses that safety is an important part of the job for employees at his company, and they take many precautions to avoid injury. Employees attend mandatory weekly safety meetings, and in his present position, Phil wears a hard hat 60 percent of the time. This is even more than he did as an installer. Employees are required to wear a hard hat whenever they climb a ladder or pole or go up in a bucket truck. They must also wear gloves and a safety belt. When working on the side of a road, workers must place cones out behind their trucks to make sure they look behind their trucks before leaving the work site. Other safety precautions include taking driving-safety classes periodically and wearing seat belts at all times in service trucks.

Job Qualifications and Training for Utility Workers

Many career opportunities are available in the public utilities industry for people with varying levels of experience and education. However, because of the variety of companies and products, skills developed in one utility may not easily transfer to another.

High school graduates can qualify for most entry-level production jobs. They begin as laborers and advance through on-the-job training or apprenticeships into higher-paying jobs that offer more responsibilities. It is possible to advance to crew leader and supervisor positions. In telecommunications, utility companies prefer equipment mechanics, installers, and repairers to have training beyond high school in electronics. Because telecommunications is rapidly introducing new technologies and services, employees need to keep their skills current to be effective in their jobs.

Bachelor's degrees in engineering are essential for entry-level positions as engineers at all utility companies. To obtain a technician position, it is usually necessary to have completed a two-year program at a community college or technical institute. To become a manager at a utility, you need a bachelor's degree or a two-year technical degree.

Job Outlook and Earnings

The employment picture is decidedly mixed for utilities. Some segments will present excellent opportunities for employment, while others will actually experience a decline in the number of employees, as seen in Table 1.

Table 1. Projected employment growth in public utilities by industry segment, 1998–2008

INDUSTRY SEGMENT	PERCENT CHANGE
Water supply and sanitary services	18.7
Electric services	-5.3
Gas production and distribution	-17.6
Telecommunications services	5.0

Source: U.S. Department of Labor, Bureau of Labor Statistics, 2007

Deregulation has increased competition in the electric and gas utilities, which has resulted in newer plants and increased productivity—and therefore a decline in employment. While regulatory changes have occurred in all segments of the utility industry, the water supply and sanitary services industries have experienced an opposite impact on employment. Regulations that increase the number of contaminants to be monitored and treated have expanded employment opportunities. Increased employment needs are directly related to the increase in the amount of waste, more stringent disposal requirements for different materials, and the percentage of refuse that is recycled. Within this segment, more truck drivers, landfill equipment operators, water and waste treatment plant operators, hazardous materials removal workers, and machinery, equipment, and motor vehicle mechanics will be needed. Employment in the telecommunications industry will also increase because of the demand for high-capacity communications. This is good news for hard-hat wearers as more line installers and repairers will be needed to upgrade existing systems and to install new ones.

In general, your earnings in a public utility will be higher than in other industries in part due to overtime and weekend work, which commands higher hourly rates. Average weekly wages overall in the utility industry for nonsupervisory workers exceed $1,136, compared to about $568 in private industry overall. The highest-paid employees work in combination utility services, followed by electric services, gas production and distribution, telecommunications, and sanitary services.

For More Information

The easiest way to find out about jobs with utility companies is to contact local companies or the unions to which their workers belong. Here are some organizations you can contact for more career information:

American Gas Association
400 North Capitol Street NW
Washington, DC 20001
www.aga.org

American Water Works Association
6666 West Quincy Avenue
Denver, CO 80235
www.awwa.org

Atlantic Canada Water Works Association
PO Box 41002
Dartmouth, NS B2Y 4P7
Canada
www.acwwa.ca

Canadian Gas Association
350 Sparks Street, Suite 809
Ottawa, ON K1R 7S8
Canada
www.cga.ca

National Cable & Telecommunications Association
25 Massachusetts Avenue NW, Suite 100
Washington, DC 20001
www.ncta.com

Society of Cable Telecommunications Engineers
140 Philips Road
Exton, PA 19341
www.scte.org

Telecommunications Workers Union
5261 Lane Street
Burnaby, BC V5H 4A6
Canada
www.twu-canada.ca

United States Telecom Association
607 Fourteenth Street NW, Suite 400
Washington, DC 20005
www.usta.org

Utility Workers Union of America
815 Sixteenth Street NW, Suite 605
Washington, DC 20006
www.uwua.net

CHAPTER NINE

More Hard-Hat Careers

I n this book, you have read about many different occupations that require workers to wear hard hats. There are still many more jobs where wearing a hard hat is essential, although you may have to be creative to find some of them. Browse through an occupational handbook, paying particular attention to the sections on working conditions, and you will discover some of them. You can further expand your list by reviewing want ads, visiting school placement offices, looking at job listings at state and federal employment information offices, visiting private employment agencies, and by searching on the Internet. Another sure way of learning what jobs require employees to wear hard hats is by noting the occupations of all the people you see wearing them. You may notice a butcher in your supermarket, a tree trimmer sawing off dead branches, a farm worker operating equipment, a shipyard worker on the deck of a ship, or a forklift operator moving boxes. In this chapter, we will tell you about a few more careers in which wearing a hard hat is required.

Elevator Installers and Repairers

There are only about thirty thousand elevator installer and repairer jobs in the United States, but this is an essential occupation because this equipment must always must be kept in good working condition. Elevator installers and repairers also assemble, install, and replace escalators, dumbwaiters, moving walkways, and similar equipment. It can be a dangerous job, involving such hazards as falls, electrical shock, muscle strains, and other injuries related to handling heavy equipment.

Elevator installers and repairers must have a thorough knowledge of electronics, electricity, and hydraulics. Most learn the trade through a program administered by local joint educational committees representing employers and the International Union of Elevator Constructors. Generally, trainees or helpers must successfully complete a six-month probationary period. It then takes from four to five years to become a fully qualified mechanic.

On the Job with a Grain Elevator Operator

A grain elevator is a tall building that stores grain. Machinery loads, unloads, cleans, and mixes the grain. Bill Stopes is a grain elevator operator. Most of his training has been on the job, but his ability to weld and perform electrical and general maintenance work from his previous job in construction has been extremely helpful. Bill usually starts his mornings cleaning because a grain elevator is extremely dirty and dusty. The rest of his day varies. During certain times of the year, Bill operates equipment that helps dump grain into the elevators. When the elevator is not too busy, he catches up on building and machine maintenance. One aspect Bill enjoys most about his job is the diversity of the work. To help avoid injuries, he wears a hard hat, eye-protection gear, and earplugs.

Firefighters

Fires destroy billions of dollars of property and take thousands of lives each year. Firefighters are the hard-hat (helmet) wearers trained to protect the public from fires by responding quickly to emergency situations. It is a dangerous career in which injuries can arise from sudden cave-ins of floors, toppling walls, traffic accidents when responding to calls, and exposure to flames, smoke, and other poisonous gases and chemicals. Fighting fires requires complex organization and teamwork. At fires, firefighters connect hose lines to hydrants, operate pumps for high-pressure hoses, and position ladders to deliver water to the fire. They also rescue victims, administer emergency medical aid as needed, ventilate smoke-filled areas, and try to salvage the contents of buildings. Firefighters also handle emergency medical services in many communities.

On the Job with a Firefighter

Nelson Smith is a volunteer firefighter who serves as a captain and maintenance officer in a small rural community. Whenever his pager goes off, he rushes down to the station, hops into his gear, and climbs aboard the fire truck. On the way, Nelson gathers all the information he can about the situation in order to plan what action will be taken when they arrive at the fire. Once there, Nelson instructs his team on how to set up to fight the fire, and he is often one of the first to go into the fire. Back at the station, Nelson has other responsibilities as the maintenance officer. He makes sure everything is in good working condition and must correct any problems. It took a great deal of training for Nelson to learn how to be a firefighter. He completed a basic medical class and passed two different firefighter courses.

Hazardous Materials Removal Workers

Hazardous materials removal workers identify, remove, package, transport, and dispose of various hazardous materials, including asbestos, lead, and radioactive and nuclear materials. You can enter this job with a high school diploma, but you must complete a training program to become licensed as a hazardous materials removal worker. Most workers continue to update their skills through classes.

In this job, you wear a hard hat, an all-encompassing protective suit, disposable or reusable coveralls, gloves, shoe covers, safety glasses or goggles, and face shields. You may also be required to wear respirators ranging from simple ones covering only the mouth and nose to self-contained suits with their own oxygen supplies. Almost forty thousand hazardous materials removal workers are employed in the United States, with about two-thirds employed by special trade contractors, primarily in asbestos and lead abatement.

Environmental Scientists

Stacey Weimer has a degree in civil engineering with an emphasis on environmental engineering. Her job is to conduct environmental assessments throughout the country. She has worked in mud lagoons, creeks, lakes, and other contaminated sites. Out on a job site, most of her fieldwork consists of collecting soil and water samples. Collecting samples can be a dirty job, so Stacey usually wears jeans, a T-shirt, and steel-toed boots. Sometimes she wears a hard hat and safety glasses.

Most of her work is completed as part of a team that includes professionals from her office, the client, and contractors. When she is not out in the field, Stacey is in her office writing and reviewing reports, researching information, and making phone calls. She also keeps abreast of current technology and advances in environmental engineering. What Stacey likes best about her career is actually seeing the end product, which is the removal of contamination and a clean site. She enjoys having a career that helps the world by reducing environmental contamination.

Police Officers

If you join the military police or become a motor patrol officer on a local or state police force, you will always wear a helmet (hard hat) on the job. Both of these jobs require special training. To become a patrol officer, you must usually be at least twenty years old, meet rigorous physical and personal qualifications, and pass competitive examinations.

To become a member of the military police, you must join the military and demonstrate that you have the qualifications to be selected for the job. The work in both occupations can be dangerous and stressful.

Forge Shop Workers

Forging involves heating metal or a combination of metals and then hammering or pressing it into a desired form. The simplest kind of forging is done by blacksmiths.

Most forged materials are made in shops filled with heavy machinery, metal objects, and furnaces containing molten metal. Hard hats and other protective gear are mandatory in forge shops to protect workers from flying, broken metal and accidents involving the machinery.

A Look at the Future

The future is bright for those who want hard-hat careers, even though machines or robots will take some of these jobs. Hard-hat workers will be required in far more occupations in the years to come because of the increasing concern for safety in the workplace.

Hard-hat jobs will always be exciting because there is an element of danger in them. Nevertheless, with proper safety precautions, most of these jobs are no more dangerous than average. The secret is to be familiar enough with the rules and regulations on your particular job that you can enjoy the excitement and still minimize or prevent any potential danger to yourself or a fellow worker.

About the Authors

Marjorie Eberts and Margaret Gisler have been writing together professionally for thirty-one years. They are prolific freelance authors with more than ninety books in print. Their publications include more than twenty career books, language arts and mathematics textbooks, advice books for parents, and children's books. Besides writing books, the two authors write the King Features syndicated "Dear Teacher" column that appears in newspapers across the United States.

Writing this book was a special pleasure for the authors as it gave them the opportunity to talk to so many hard-hat wearers, including several in their families. They appreciate the value these people place on working safely in jobs where there are dangers in the workplace.

Marjorie Eberts has a bachelor and master's degree from Stanford University, and Margaret Gisler has her bachelor and doctoral degrees from Ball State University and her master's from Butler University. Both received their specialist degrees in education from Butler University.